Venice
TRIVIA

500 QUESTIONS

Jim McLain

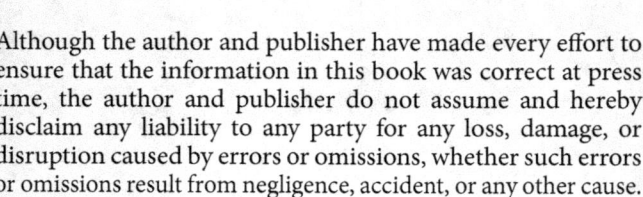

Printed in the United States of America

First Printing July 2022

ISBN 978-1-956661-09-5 Paperback
ISBN 978-1-956661-10-1 Hardcover

Published by:

Book Services
www.BookServices.us

1. If you are in room 201 of a hotel in Venice, what floor are you on?
   a. 1st
   b. 2nd
   c. 3rd
   d. 4th

2. The Doge's Palace was the home of the most powerful men in Venice for about how many years?
   a. 400
   b. 500
   c. 600
   d. 700

3. Who wrote "I stood in Venice, on the Bridge of Sighs, a palace and a prison on each hand"?
   a. Casanova
   b. Lord Byron
   c. Marco Polo
   d. Emma Lazarus

4. About what years did the Doges rule Venice?
   a. 1100 - 1450
   b. 1150 – 1550
   c. 1200 - 1600
   d. 1250 - 1750

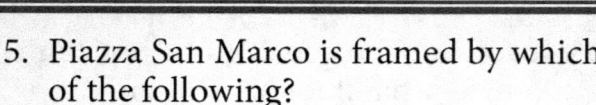

5. Piazza San Marco is framed by which of the following?
    a. The Doge's Palace
    b. The waterfront
    c. The Library
    d. All of the above

6. What color is the Doge's Palace?
    a. White
    b. Ivory
    c. Pale pink
    d. Bright pink

7. What is on top of one of the two columns by the waterfront of St. Mark's Square?
    a. A torch
    b. St. Mark's winged lion
    c. Sword
    d. Vase

8. Murano is famous for which industry?
    a. Glass blowing
    b. Lacemaking
    c. Furniture
    d. Ship building

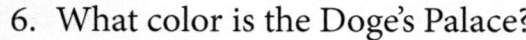
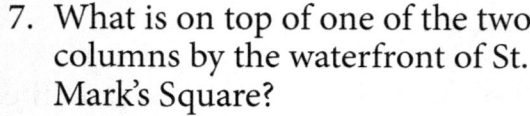

9. Burano is famous for which industry?
   a. Glass blowing
   b. Lacemaking
   c. Furniture
   d. Ship building

10. Torcello has a population of about how many?
    a. 20
    b. 30
    c. 40
    d. 50

11. Torcello is the site of Venice's oldest church. What is famous about this church?
    a. Madonna and Child painting
    b. Crucifixion painting
    c. The Last Judgment mosaic
    d. Twelve Apostle mosaic

12. St. Mark's is modeled after which church?
    a. Church of Christ the King
    b. Church of the Holy Apostles
    c. Church of Mary
    d. Church of the Conception

13. St. Mark is the author of what?
   a. The Lord's Prayer
   b. The Nicene Creed
   c. One of the four gospels
   d. The Gloria

14. Eight centuries after the death of St. Mark, who rescued his body?
   a. The Italian Army
   b. Two visiting merchants from Venice
   c. The Pope's Guards
   d. King Charles

15. In what year was St. Mark's body rescued?
   a. 765 AD
   b. 801 AD
   c. 829 AD
   d. 851 AD

16. From where was St. Mark's body rescued?
   a. Cairo, Egypt
   b. Alexandria, Egypt
   c. Constantinople, Turkey
   d. Athens, Greece

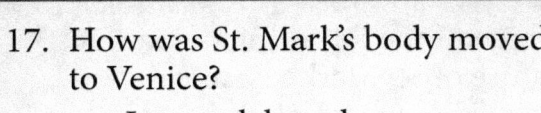

17. How was St. Mark's body moved to Venice?

    a. In a pork barrel
    b. In an olive wood casket
    c. In a large ceramic jug
    d. None of the above

18. When St. Mark's body was moved to Venice, to whom was it presented?

    a. The Pope
    b. The Bishop
    c. The Doge
    d. The Cardinal

19. St. Mark's original church burnt down in what year?

    a. 958
    b. 976
    c. 989
    d. 996

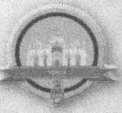

20. The structure we see today of St. Mark's Basilica was started in what year?

    a. 947
    b. 982
    c. 1025
    d. 1063

21. Which of the following is a famous feature of St. Mark's Basilica?
    a. Its four bronze horses
    b. Its onion domes
    c. Its columns
    d. All of the above

22. St. Mark's Basilica was modeled after which of the following?
    a. The Vatican
    b. A church in Constantinople
    c. Notre Dame
    d. The Church of Mary and Child

23. About how many yards of mosaics are on the walls of St. Mark's?
    a. 2,000
    b. 3,000
    c. 4,000
    d. 5,000

24. St. Mark's has iconic images of Mary and of Christ Pantocrator, which means what?
    a. God's Son
    b. Ruler of all things
    c. The crucified
    d. The ascended

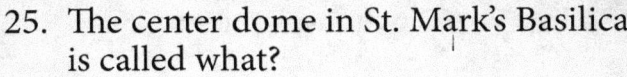

25. The center dome in St. Mark's Basilica is called what?

    a. The Ascension Mosaic
    b. The Creation Dome
    c. The Pentecost Dome
    d. The Dome of St. Mark

26. St. Mark's Basilica is a series of perfect circles within perfect squares. What does this arrangement represent?

    a. Geometric design
    b. Mathematical balance
    c. The cosmic order
    d. Harmony

27. The pulpit to the right of the main altar in St. Mark's was reserved for whom?

    a. The Pope
    b. The Doge
    c. The Cardinal
    d. The lay minister

28. In the north transept in St. Mark's is an icon of Mary and baby Jesus called the Nicopeia. What does Nicopeia mean?

    a. Holy Child
    b. Servant of God
    c. Our Lady of Victory
    d. Virgin and Child

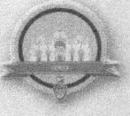

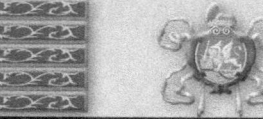

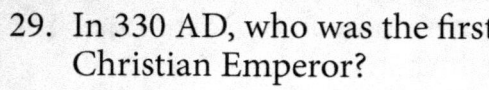

29. In 330 AD, who was the first
    Christian Emperor?
    a. Caesar
    b. Nicholas
    c. Justine
    d. Constantine

30. In what year did the Doge
    let crusaders loot the city
    of Constantinople?
    a. 1204
    b. 1220
    c. 1252
    d. 1287

31. Which booty did the crusaders bring
    to the Doge at the Piazza San Marco?
    a. Bronze Horses
    b. Bronze doors from Hagia Sophia
    c. The Nicopeia icon
    d. All of the above

32. In the south transept of St. Mark's
    is a mosaic of the last supper. What
    material was used to reflect the light?
    a. Silver
    b. Palladium
    c. Gold
    d. None of the above

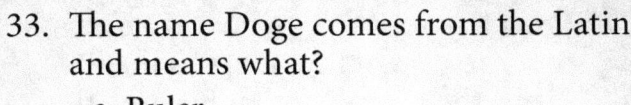

33. The name Doge comes from the Latin and means what?
    a. Ruler
    b. Supreme
    c. Leader
    d. Almighty

34. In 1094, St. Mark's Basilica was almost complete. St. Mark's bones had been stored and no one remembered where they were located. Where were they found?
    a. In a pork barrel
    b. In the rubble from construction
    c. Inside a hollow column
    d. Under the steps by the altar

35. The treasury of St. Mark's holds a collection of items stolen from where?
    a. Athens
    b. Constantinople
    c. Alexandria
    d. Rome

36. In about what year did St. Mark die?
    a. 52 AD
    b. 59 AD
    c. 61 AD
    d. 68 AD

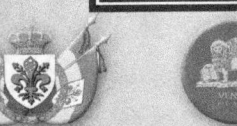

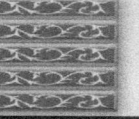

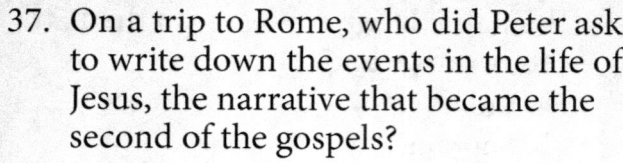

37. On a trip to Rome, who did Peter ask to write down the events in the life of Jesus, the narrative that became the second of the gospels?

    a. Matthew
    b. Mark
    c. Luke
    d. John

38. During his travels, Mark dreamed of a Latin-speaking angel, who said "pax tibi Marce, evangelista meus." Which means?

    a. My evangelist, Mark
    b. Peace be with you, Mark
    c. Peace to you, Mark, my evangelist
    d. My evangelist, Mark, peace be with you

39. How did Mark die?

    a. At the hands of a mob
    b. At the hands of anti-Christians
    c. He was tied and dragged through the streets
    d. All of the above

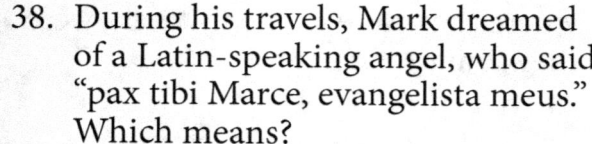

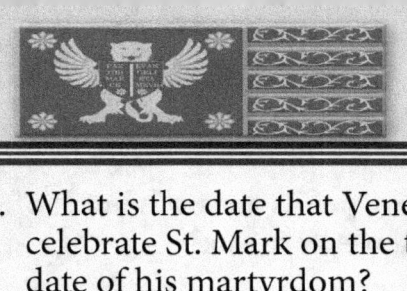

40. What is the date that Venetians celebrate St. Mark on the traditional date of his martyrdom?
    a. January 25
    b. March 25
    c. April 25
    d. May 25

41. As promised by an angel, Mark rests in peace under a golden altar inscribed with "Corpus Divi Marci Evangelistae," which means what?
    a. Evangelist Mark, rest in peace
    b. Rest in peace, Mark the evangelist
    c. Body of the Evangelist Mark
    d. Evangelist Mark's body

42. The Golden Altarpiece is a wall of how many blue-backed enamels of religious themes?
    a. 175
    b. 200
    c. 225
    d. 250

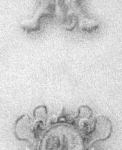

43. How many rubies are in the wall of the Golden Altarpiece?
    a. 9
    b. 12
    c. 15
    d. 18

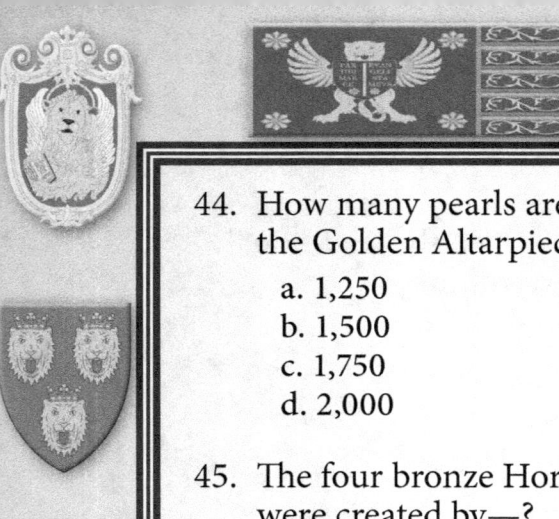

44. How many pearls are in the wall of the Golden Altarpiece?
    a. 1,250
    b. 1,500
    c. 1,750
    d. 2,000

45. The four bronze Horses of St. Mark were created by—?
    a. Hammering
    b. Bending
    c. Casting in clay molds
    d. All the above

46. The four bronze Horses of St. Mark contain what percent of copper?
    a. 85%
    b. 91%
    c. 97%
    d. 99%

47. What are the eyes of the four Horses of St. Mark?
    a. Rubies
    b. Emeralds
    c. Diamonds
    d. Pearls

48. Legend says the four bronze Horses of St. Mark were made for whom?

    a. Napoleon
    b. Alexander the Great
    c. Constantine
    d. Caesar

49. When were the four horses brought into St. Mark's?

    a. 1209
    b. 1221
    c. 1245
    d. 1255

50. What describes the heads of the four horses at St. Mark's Basilica?

    a. Detachable
    b. Adjustable
    c. Swappable
    d. All of the above

51. When the Doge wanted to address the crowds outdoors, where did he stand?

    a. In the center of St. Mark's Piazza
    b. Between the four horses
    c. At the traditional entrance to the Doge's Palace
    d. Between the two columns at the water entrance

52. Why were the four horses moved inside?
    a. The threat of theft
    b. The threat of vandalism
    c. The threat of oxidation
    d. All of the above

53. In what year were the four horses moved inside from the balcony of St. Mark's?
    a. 1970
    b. 1975
    c. 1987
    d. 1990

54. Who stole the four horses and moved them to Paris?
    a. King Charles
    b. Napoleon
    c. French General Francis Lannes
    d. French General Joseph Berthier

55. Venice's Grand Canal is about how long?
    a. 1 mile
    b. 2 miles
    c. 3 miles
    d. 4 miles

56. Venice's Grand Canal is nearly how wide?
    a. 100 feet
    b. 125 feet
    c. 150 feet
    d. 175 feet

57. Venice's Grand Canal is nearly how deep?
    a. 10 feet
    b. 15 feet
    c. 20 feet
    d. 25 feet

58. Venice's Casino is in a palace where German composer Richard Wagner died in what year?
    a. 1880
    b. 1881
    c. 1882
    d. 1883

59. The Rialto Bridge was built in what year?
    a. 1577
    b. 1582
    c. 1588
    d. 1591

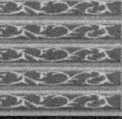

60. The Rialto Bridge is the _____ one built on the same spot?

    a. 2nd

    b. 3rd

    c. 4th

    d. 5th

61. In what decade was the original Rialto Bridge, the first one to cross the Grand Canal, built?

    a. 1150s

    b. 1160s

    c. 1170s

    d. 1180s

62. How far do the foundations extend on either side of the Rialto Bridge?

    a. 500 feet

    b. 550 feet

    c. 600 feet

    d. 650 feet

63. What is the shape of La Salute church dome?

    a. Crown-shaped dome

    b. Pointed dome

    c. Square dome

    d. Eight-sided dome

64. La Salute church was built to thank God for what blessing?

   a. Venetian wealth

   b. Bringing fresh water to Venice

   c. Saving Venetians from the plague

   d. All of the above

65. In what year did the plague kill about 1/3 of the population of Venice?

   a. 1600

   b. 1610

   c. 1620

   d. 1630

66. In 1450, Venice had a population of about how many?

   a. 150,000

   b. 180,000

   c. 195,000

   d. 210,000

67. How tall is the Campanile Tower in St. Mark's Piazza?

   a. 300 feet

   b. 312 feet

   c. 325 feet

   d. 337

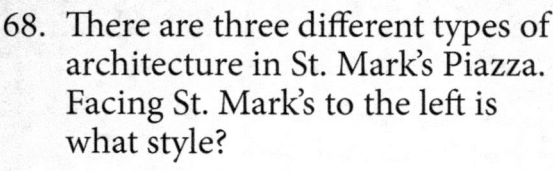

68. There are three different types of architecture in St. Mark's Piazza. Facing St. Mark's to the left is what style?

   a. High Renaissance
   b. Columns and Arch Renaissance
   c. Napoleonic
   d. Neoclassical

69. There are three different types of architecture in St. Mark's Piazza. Facing St. Mark's to the right is what style?

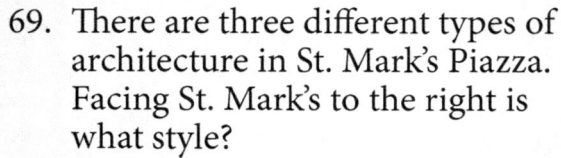

   a. High Renaissance
   b. Columns and Arch Renaissance
   c. Napoleonic
   d. Neoclassical

70. At the opposite end of St. Mark's Piazza is what type of architecture?

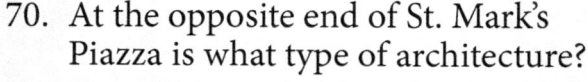

   a. Buildings designed to fit in
   b. Neoclassical
   c. High Renaissance
   d. Columns and Arch Renaissance

71. To the left side, facing St. Mark's, is which building?

   a. New Procurators' Offices
   b. Napoleonic-style buildings
   c. Old Procurators' Offices
   d. Doge's Palace

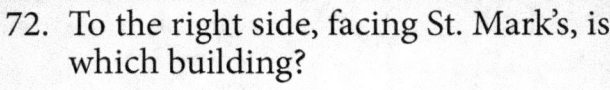

72. To the right side, facing St. Mark's, is which building?
    a. Clock tower
    b. "Old Offices"
    c. Napoleon-style buildings
    d. New Procurators'Offices

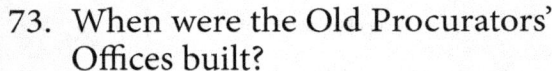

73. When were the Old Procurators' Offices built?
    a. About 1500
    b. About 1400
    c. About 1300
    d. About 1200

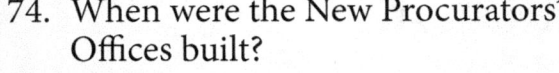

74. When were the New Procurators' Offices built?
    a. About 1400
    b. About 1500
    c. About 1600
    d. About 1700

75. When wasNapoleon's wing added to the Piazza?
    a. 1500s
    b. 1600s
    c. 1700s
    d. 1800s

19

76. Which is not an order of columns?
   a. Doric
   b. Ionic
   c. Corinthian
   d. Aegean

77. St. Mark's Square is in the exact center of the—?
   a. North-South axis
   b. Southern Meridian
   c. East-West axis
   d. Northern Meridian

78. What is called the "wine of Islam"?
   a. Coffee
   b. Wine
   c. Olive oil
   d. Opium

79. St. Mark's Basilica is a mix of East and West. Which of the following can be found there?
   a. Muslim-style domes
   b. Roman-style arches over the doorways
   c. Pointed Gothic pinnacles
   d. All of the above

80. What two bronze sculptures stand atop the clock tower in St. Mark's Piazza?
    a. Lions
    b. Moors
    c. Anvils
    d. Fish

81. What is on the clock tower in St. Mark's Piazza?
    a. Signs of the Zodiac
    b. Phases of the moon
    c. A clock dial showing 24 hours
    d. All of the above

82. Venice became the richest city from trade with which of the following?
    a. Ottoman Muslims
    b. Byzantine Christians
    c. Europeans
    d. All of the above

83. The original Campanile (bell tower) toppled into St. Mark's Piazza in what year?
    a. 1899
    b. 1902
    c. 1905
    d. 1908

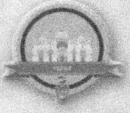

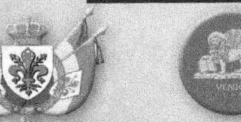

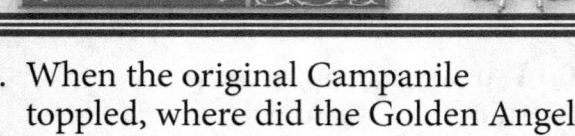

84. When the original Campanile toppled, where did the Golden Angel on the top land?

    a. On the clock tower
    b. Toward the Old Offices
    c. At the Basilica's front door
    d. Toward the New Offices

85. When the Campanile Tower fell, the Golden Angel landed in what position?

    a. Facing left
    b. Facing right
    c. Face down
    d. Standing upright

86. After the collapse of the Campanile Tower, how many years did it take to rebuild it?

    a. 9
    b. 10
    c. 11
    d. 12

87. What is the name of the Archangel at the top of the Campanile Tower?

    a. Gabriel
    b. Michael
    c. Anthony
    d. Francis

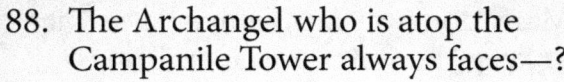

88. The Archangel who is atop the Campanile Tower always faces—?

    a. North
    b. South
    c. The breeze
    d. None of the above

89. To prevent a repeat of the Campanile Tower collapse, a titanium girdle was added in about what year?

    a. 1970
    b. 1990
    c. 2010
    d. 2020

90. During flooding in St. Mark's piazza, how do people get from one side to the other?

    a. Portable wooden walkways
    b. They don't cross
    c. They get wet
    d. None of the above

91. In what year were the pavers in St. Mark's Piazza taken up and raised by adding a layer of sand?

    a. 2004
    b. 2005
    c. 2006
    d. 2007

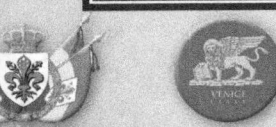

92. Many doorways in Venice have what to keep the water out of buildings?
    a. Low wooden or metal barriers
    b. Steel doors
    c. Wooden doors
    d. Sandbags

93. How effective are the devices used to keep the water out of buildings in Venice?
    a. Highly effective
    b. Moderately effective
    c. Slightly effective
    d. Not effective

94. At the lagoon entrance to St. Mark's Piazza stand two columns from which century?
    a. 10th
    b. 11th
    c. 12th
    d. 13th

95. At the lagoon entrance to St. Mark's Piazza, what is atop one of the columns?
    a. St. Mark's winged lion
    b. A fish
    c. A sword
    d. A key

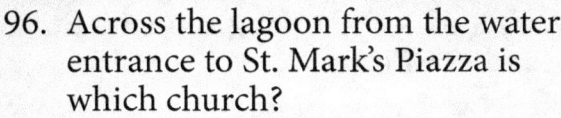

96. Across the lagoon from the water entrance to St. Mark's Piazza is which church?

    a. La Salute Church
    b. Church of San Zaccaria
    c. Church of San Polo
    d. Church of the San Giorgio Maggiore

97. Who is the architect who designed the church across from the water entrance to St. Mark's Piazza?

    a. Andrea Palladio
    b. Gian Lorenzo Bernini
    c. Filippo Brunelleschi
    d. Giorgio Vasari

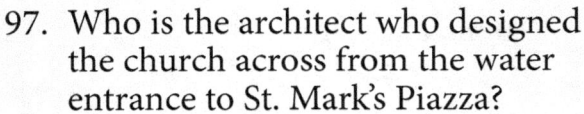

98. Scuola San Rocco is called "Tintoretto's Sistine Chapel." Which famous painting is upstairs in a small room?

    a. Madonna and Child
    b. Crucifixion
    c. Last Supper
    d. The Apostles

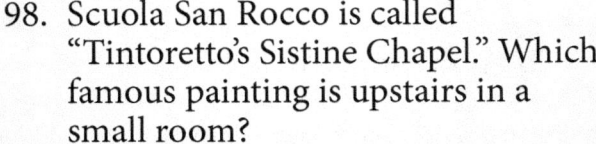
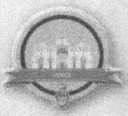

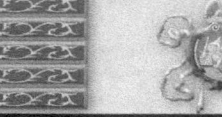

99. Which of the following is not on St. Mark's Basilica?
    a. Byzantine mosaics
    b. Muslim onion domes
    c. Gothic pinnacles
    d. The Tablecloth

100. St. Mark's Basilica is a brick structure covered in marble that was looted from what city?
    a. Constantinople
    b. Alexandria
    c. Athens
    d. Rome

101. Where did the columns at St. Mark's Basilica came from?
    a. Alexandria
    b. Athens
    c. Cairo
    d. Constantinople

102. Where did the capitals on the columns at St. Mark's Basilica came from?
    a. Rome
    b. Athens
    c. Sicily
    d. Cairo

103. The carvings on the columns at St. Mark's Basilica came from?
    a. Constantinople
    b. Athens
    c. Rome
    d. Anatolia

104. The clock tower at St. Mark's Piazza was originally built in what year?
    a. 1458
    b. 1499
    c. 1506
    d. 1528

105. The winged lion on the clock tower in St. Mark's piazza has an open book in which is written *Pax tibi Marce*. What does that mean?
    a. Be safe, Mark
    b. Safe travels, Mark
    c. Peace be with you, Mark
    d. All the above

106. The digital clock on the clock tower in St. Mark's Piazza changes every how many minutes?
    a. 1
    b. 3
    c. 5
    d. 10

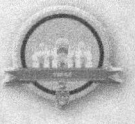

107. What does the winged
lion symbolize?

    a. St. Mark
    b. Italy
    c. World trade
    d. None of the above

108. What is the highest recorded flood
level in St. Mark's Piazza?

    a. 53 inches
    b. 61 inches
    c. 77 inches
    d. 82 inches

109. In what year was the highest flood
level recorded in St. Mark's Piazza?

    a. 1966
    b. 1968
    c. 1970
    d. 1972

110. Venice had a high tide in December
2008 of how many inches?

    a. 41
    b. 48
    c. 56
    d. 61

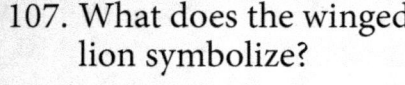

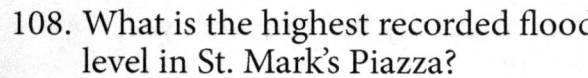

111. At the traditional entrance to the Doge's Palace is a statue with how many roman soldiers?

    a. 2
    b. 4
    c. 6
    d. 8

112. At the traditional entrance to the Doge's Palace is a statue of Roman soldiers. What are they called?

    a. Tetrarchs
    b. Guards
    c. Manets
    d. Protectors

113. The seventh column at the Doge's Palace is a carved capital depicting which of the following?

    a. Story of Love
    b. Story of Romance
    c. Story of Tragedy
    d. All the above

114. What is the name of the bridge that connects the Doge Palace and the prison?

    a. Bridge of Sighs
    b. Ponte del Rialto
    c. Accademia
    d. Ponte dei Pugni

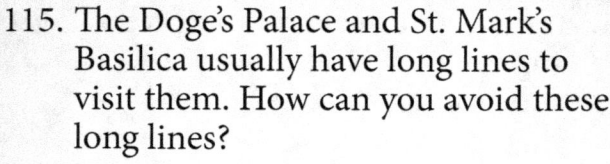

115. The Doge's Palace and St. Mark's Basilica usually have long lines to visit them. How can you avoid these long lines?

    a. Get there early
    b. Purchase a ticket ahead of time
    c. Get there late
    d. All the above

116. The mosaic over the far-left door of St. Mark's Basilica shows what?

    a. The coffin of St. Mark
    b. The Virgin Mary
    c. Jesus ascending into heaven
    d. The Twelve Apostles

117. St. Mark's is a–?

    a. Basilica
    b. Cathedral
    c. Church
    d. All of the above

118. The four horses (which are copies) on the balcony of St. Mark's Basilica were looted from where?

    a. Rhodes
    b. Constantinople
    c. Athens
    d. Cairo

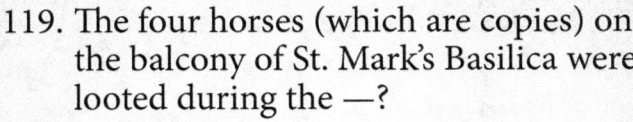

119. The four horses (which are copies) on the balcony of St. Mark's Basilica were looted during the —?

    a. Second crusade
    b. Third crusade
    c. Fourth Crusade
    d. Fifth Crusade

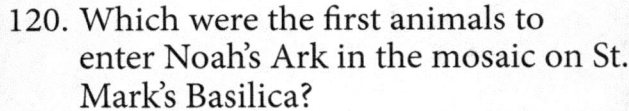

120. Which were the first animals to enter Noah's Ark in the mosaic on St. Mark's Basilica?

    a. Lions
    b. Elephants
    c. Zebras
    d. Cows

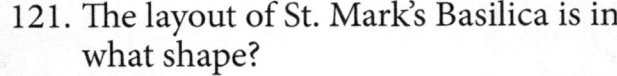

121. The layout of St. Mark's Basilica is in what shape?

    a. Greek Cross
    b. Roman Cross
    c. Five-star Cross
    d. Cysteine Cross

122. The Pentecost Mosaics in St. Mark's Basilica show the Apostles receiving what?

    a. The ability to speak in other languages
    b. The written word of God
    c. The virtues
    d. The beatitudes

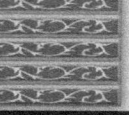

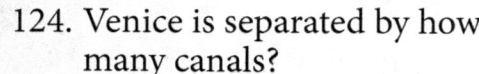

123. Venice rests on how many islands?
    a. 96
    b. 101
    c. 112
    d. 118

124. Venice is separated by how many canals?
    a. 147
    b. 150
    c. 153
    d. 158

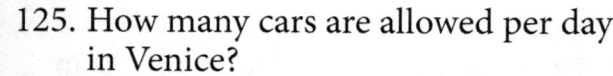

125. How many cars are allowed per day in Venice?
    a. 0
    b. 10
    c. 25
    d. 50

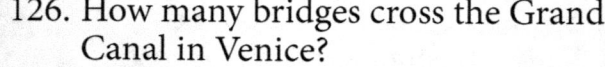

126. How many bridges cross the Grand Canal in Venice?
    a. 1
    b. 2
    c. 3
    d. 4

127. In its day, Venice was extremely wealthy from trade due to its location with connections to what region?
   a. Europe
   b. Central Asia
   c. Middle East
   d. All of the above

128. Marco Polo was a Venetian born in what year?
   a. 1254
   b. 1258
   c. 1262
   d. 1264

129. About how many gondolas are there in Venice?
   a. 350
   b. 400
   c. 450
   d. 500

130. How many footbridges are there in Venice?
   a. 336
   b. 389
   c. 401
   d. 417

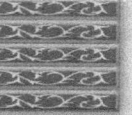

131. How many private footbridges are there in Venice?

    a. 64
    b. 67
    c. 72
    d. 78

132. Which of the following is a wooden bridge in Venice?

    a. Ponte Dell' Accademia
    b. Ponte Degli Scalzi
    c. Ponte Della Constituzione
    d. Ponte di Calatrava

133. How many years did Marco Polo live abroad?

    a. 15
    b. 17
    c. 21
    d. 24

134. Marco Polo was imprisoned in which city?

    a. Genoa
    b. Athens
    c. Rhodes
    d. Phira

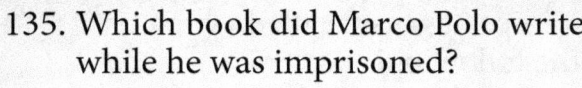

135. Which book did Marco Polo write
while he was imprisoned?
   - a. *The Travels of Marco Polo*
   - b. *The History of Greece*
   - c. *The History of Italy*
   - d. *The Emperors of Rome*

136. The Rialto Market in Venice is nearly
how many years old?
   - a. 500
   - b. 750
   - c. 1,000
   - d. 1,250

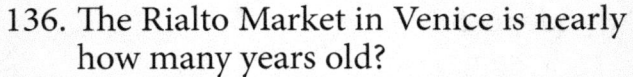

137. The Rialto Bridge dates from
which year?
   - a. 1140
   - b. 1160
   - c. 1180
   - d. 1200

138. Venice has been called which of
the following?
   - a. City of Canals
   - b. The floating City
   - c. Serenissima
   - d. All of the above

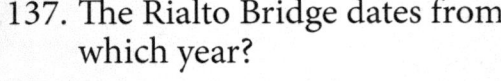

139. Venice has been called which of the following?
   a. Queen of the Adriatic
   b. City of Water
   c. City of Bridges
   d. All of the above

140. How much did it cost for a Gondola ride in 2021?
   a. 60 Euros
   b. 70
   c. 80 Euros
   d. 90

141. About how much did a Venetian gondolier earn a year in U.S. dollars in 2021?
   a. $75,000
   b. $100,000
   c. $125,000
   d. $150,000

142. Between 697 and 1797 Venice was known as what?
   a. The Republic of Venice
   b. The Kingdom of Venice
   c. The State of Venice
   d. The United Islands of Venice

143. How many churches are there in Venice?

    a. 141

    b. 143

    c. 147

    d. 151

144. Which is the oldest church in Venice?

    a. Santi Apostoli

    b. San Giacomo di Rialto

    c. San Nicolo dei Mendicoli

    d. San Giorgio Maggiore

145. San Giacomo di Rialto may have begun building in what year?

    a. 387

    b. 416

    c. 421

    d. 435

146. The inscription on the gothic porch of San Giacomo di Rialto encourages merchants of the Rialto market to be?

    a. Honest and Loyal

    b. Happy

    c. In tune with God

    d. All of the above

147. The Church of Santi Apostoli is named after–?

    a. The 12 Apostles
    b. St. Mark
    c. St. Peter
    d. St. Paul

148. The Church of San Nicolo dei Mendicoli was built in which century?

    a. 5th
    b. 6th
    c. 7th
    d. 8th

149. What does "mendicoli" mean?

    a. Wealthy
    b. Poor
    c. Upper class
    d. Lower class

150. The mosaic over the far-left door of St. Mark's Basilica shows two men holding what in their hands?

    a. Crooked staffs
    b. Gifts
    c. The Bible
    d. None of the above

151. The rich Venetians taught Europe about the good life with which of the following?

    a. Spices
    b. Silks
    c. Jewels
    d. All of the above

152. The Church of San Polo was built in which century?

    a. 8th
    b. 9th
    c. 10th
    d. 11th

153. The church of San Polo features the works of which artists?

    a. Tintoretto
    b. Veronese
    c. Tiepolo
    d. All of the above

154. Venice's Jewish population once lived in which district?

    a. Castello
    b. Dorsoduro
    c. Guidecca
    d. Cannaregio

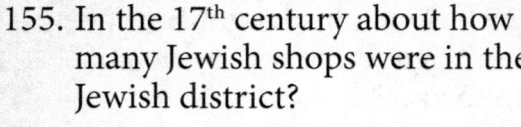

155. In the 17th century about how many Jewish shops were in the Jewish district?

    a. 60
    b. 70
    c. 80
    d. 90

156. The Jewish community center is flanked by how many Holocaust memorials?

    a. 2
    b. 3
    c. 4
    d. 5

157. During World War II about how many Jews were rounded up by the Nazis for deportation?

    a. 100
    b. 150
    c. 200
    d. 250

158. Of the Jews deported by the Nazis during World War II, how many returned?

    a. 8
    b. 10
    c. 12
    d. 14

159. How many synagogues are in the Jewish district?

    a. 3
    b. 5
    c. 7
    d. 9

160. The square in the Jewish district has how many cistern wells?

    a. 1
    b. 2
    c. 3
    d. 4

161. Jews were not allowed to live in Venice until what year?

    a. 1385
    b. 1395
    c. 1405
    d. 1415

162. What was the population of Jews in the 1600s?

    a. 3,000
    b. 4,000
    c. 5,000
    d. 6,000

163. When the population of Jews increased in the area allotted to them, they built skyscrapers of how many stories?

    a. 5
    b. 6
    c. 7
    d. 8

164. With space at a premium in the Jewish district, where were synagogues built?

    a. Over the canals
    b. Atop the skyscrapers
    c. Beneath the shops
    d. All of the above

165. How many synagogues are still active in the Jewish district?

    a. 1
    b. 2
    c. 3
    d. 4

166. How many bridges, which were locked at night, entered the Jewish district in the 1600s?

    a. 1
    b. 2
    c. 3
    d. 4

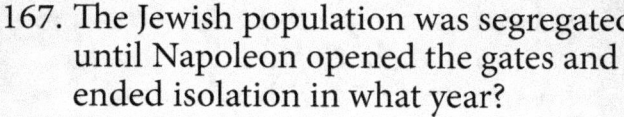

167. The Jewish population was segregated until Napoleon opened the gates and ended isolation in what year?
    a. 1795
    b. 1796
    c. 1797
    d. 1798

168. Who is the Spanish architect who designed the Ponte della Costituzione bridge?
    a. Santiago Calatrava
    b. Antoni Gaudí
    c. César Manrique)
    d. Rafael Moneo

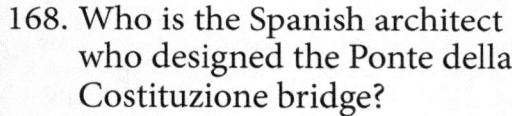

169. What was the original price of construction of the Ponte della Costituzione bridge?
    a. 6.7 million Euros
    b. 7 million Euros
    c. 8 million Euros
    d. 9 million Euros

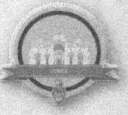

170. What was the final cost to construct the Ponte della Costituzione bridge?
    a. 10 million Euors
    b. 11 million Euros
    c. 12 million Euros
    d. 13 million Euros

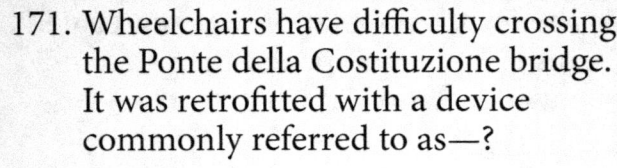

171. Wheelchairs have difficulty crossing the Ponte della Costituzione bridge. It was retrofitted with a device commonly referred to as—?
    a. The orb
    b. Stuck on the track
    c. The egg cabin
    d. The Slicker

172. Ca' d'Oro is called the palace of what?
    a. Excess
    b. Lesser painters
    c. Gold
    d. Stolen paintings

173. Scuola Dalmata de San Giorgio contains the world's best paintings of Vittoria Carpaccio, who lived in what years?
    a. 1385 - 1456
    b. 1465 - 1526
    c. 1468 - 1521
    d. 1498 - 1531

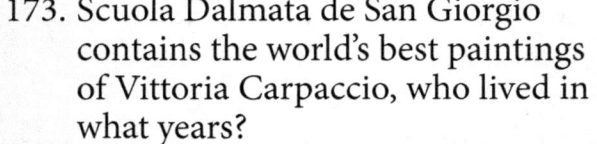

174. In the Scuola Dalmata de San Giorgio the Dalmatians held meetings and preserved their culture. Where did the Dalmatians come from?

    a. Present day Slovenia
    b. Present day Croatia
    c. Present day Montenegro
    d. Crete

175. Carpaccio was hired to paint in the chapel of Scuola Dalmata di San Giorgio in which years?

    a. 1489 - 1496
    b. 1498 - 1502
    c. 1502 – 1507
    d. 1152 – 1560

176. Which of Dalmatia's patron saints slew the dragon and metaphorically conquered paganism?

    a. St. Mark
    b. St. Francis
    c. St. Paul
    d. St. George

177. The Republic of Venice was the first great military-industrial complex to build what?
    a. Steam engines
    b. Automobiles
    c. Warships
    d. Steel railroad tracks

178. Technically, Venice has only how many canals?
    a. 3
    b. 9
    c. 15
    d. 18

179. How many canals (rivers) discharge their water into the Grand Canal?
    a. 33
    b. 37
    c. 41
    d. 45

180. The Grand Canal is lined with palaces with frescos in which colors?
    a. Reds and blues
    b. Black and white
    c. Gold leaf trim
    d. All of the above

181. Ferrovia, where the first train station was built, has been the gateway to Venice since what year?
    a. 1855
    b. 1860
    c. 1865
    d. 1870

182. Before a causeway was built to Venice, it did not have which of the following?
    a. Road access
    b. Train access
    c. A water system
    d. All of the above

183. About how many people commute daily to Venice by car, bus, or train?
    a. 10,000
    b. 15,000
    c. 20,000
    d. 25,000

184. Venice can be accessed from the train station over which bridge?
    a. Calatrava
    b. Rialto
    c. Accademia
    d. La Panda

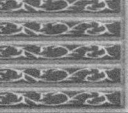

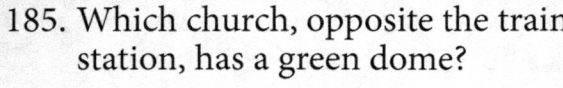

185. Which church, opposite the train station, has a green dome?

    a. Church of the Theater
    b. Sant' Angelo
    c. San Simeon Piccolo
    d. La Salute

186. Church of the Scalzi is where the last Doge rests. It was bombed by the Austrians in what year?

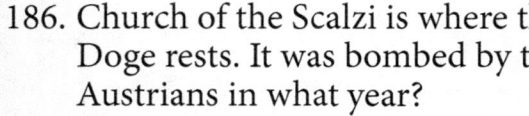

    a. 1915
    b. 1916
    c. 1917
    d. 1918

187. After the Austrians bombed the Church of the Scalizi who had it rebuilt?

    a. The Doge
    b. The Vatican
    c. Mussolini
    d. City of Venice

188. At the Church of the Scalizi what were the Carmelite monks famous for?

    a. Candlemaking
    b. Going barefoot
    c. Leather work
    d. Pottery

189. The Church of San Marcuola is only one of how many churches fronting the grand Canal?

    a. 2
    b. 3
    c. 4
    d. 5

190. The Turkish Exchange is one of the oldest houses in Venice. It features which of the following?

    a. Horseshoe arches
    b. Roofline of triangles
    c. Dingle balls
    d. All of the above

191. Along the Grand Canal, the Casino is the tallest building. What is its distinguishing feature?

    a. Columns stolen from Egypt
    b. A red canopy
    c. No two columns are identical
    d. All of the above

192. San Stae Church has which of the following features?

    a. Baroque facade
    b. No ornamentation
    c. A broken column
    d. Unfinished mosaics

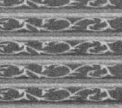

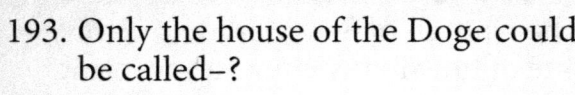

193. Only the house of the Doge could be called–?

- a. Ca'
- b. Casa
- c. House
- d. Palace

194. Ca' d'Oro is the best example of which type of architecture?

- a. Baroque
- b. Classical
- c. Venetian gothic
- d. High Renaissance

195. Venetian Gothic is a mixture of which elements?

- a. Pointed arches
- b. Round medallions
- c. Four-leaf clovers
- d. All of the above

196. Byzantine architecture exhibits which of the following?

- a. Narrow arches
- b. Tall arches
- c. Islamic frills
- d. All of the above

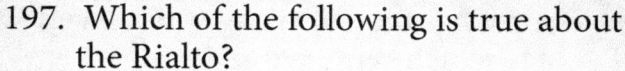

197. Which of the following is true about the Rialto?
    a. In the early days of Venice, it was a separate town
    b. It's a commercial district
    c. The Mercerie (street) connects San Marco with the Rialto
    d. All of the above

198. The merchants' palaces were multifunctional. Which of the following is true of them?
    a. The ground floor was a warehouse
    b. Offices and showrooms were upstairs
    c. Living quarters with large windows were above the offices
    d. All of the above

199. The trunks of what type of tree were used for the posts that hold up Venice?
    a. Mahogany
    b. Oak
    c. Maple
    d. Alder

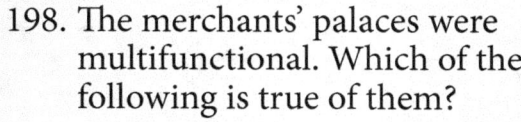

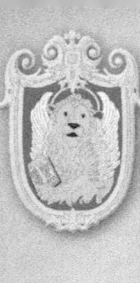

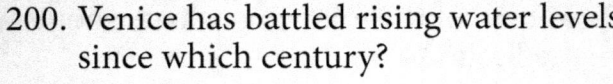

200. Venice has battled rising water levels since which century?

    a. 5th
    b. 12th
    c. 15th
    d. 19th

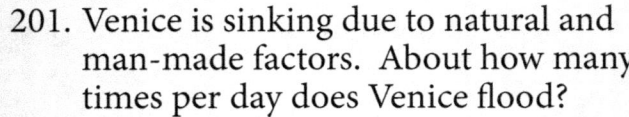

201. Venice is sinking due to natural and man-made factors. About how many times per day does Venice flood?

    a. 50
    b. 75
    c. 100
    d. 125

202. What time of the year do most floods in Venice occur?

    a. Spring (February – May)
    b. Summer (June – September)
    c. Fall/Winter (October – January)
    d. Anytime

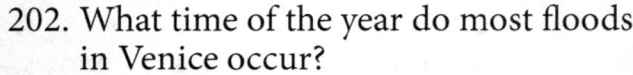

203. Venice sits atop sediments deposited at the mouth of which ancient river?

    a. Piave
    b. Po
    c. Verona
    d. Adige

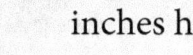

204. In the last century, about how many inches has Venice sunk?

    a. 5
    b. 7
    c. 9
    d. 11

205. Several thousand cisterns around Venice provided fresh water until what year?

    a. 1884
    b. 1888
    c. 1892
    d. 1896

206. In what year was the aqueduct completed to provide Venice with fresh water from the mountains?

    a. 1884
    b. 1888
    c. 1892
    d. 1896

207. After the flooding that occurred in 1it took until what year to come up with a solution?

    a. 2000
    b. 2003
    c. 2006
    d. 2009

208. Underwater mobile gates have been installed at how many points to keep the Adriatic from flooding Venice?

    a. 1
    b. 2
    c. 3
    d. 4

209. What is the acronym for the project to keep flood waters out of Venice?

    a. MARK
    b. MOSES
    c. MICHAEL
    d. MOSE

210. How much did it cost to travel by water taxi from Marco Polo airport to St. Mark's Piazza in 2021?

    a. 100 euros
    b. 150 euros
    c. 175 euros
    d. 200 euros

211. At the Clock Tower in St. Mark's Piazza, two Moors swing their clappers. In what century did they hit a worker, causing him to fall to his death?

    a. 15
    b. 16
    c. 17
    d. 18

212. The Doge's Palace was the seat of government for 400 years. What has it been called?

    a. The most powerful acre and a half in Europe
    b. The most powerful acre in Europe
    b. The most powerful three-fourths acre in Europe
    c. The most powerful half acre in Europe

213. The Doge's Palace was built to show off Venice's_____?

    a. Great wealth
    b. Power
    c. International trading capabilities
    d. All of the above

214. What floor of the Doge's Palace did the Doge and his family live on?

    a. Ground floor

    b. First floor up

    c. Second floor up

    d. Third floor up

215. What does the Correr Museum at St. Mark's Piazza contain that relates to the Doges?

    a. Armor

    b. Banners

    c. Statues

    d. All of the above

216. In which century did Venice decline in wealth and power?

    a. 15th

    b. 16th

    c. 17th

    d. 18th

217. La Fenice Opera House was one of how many in the 18th century?

    a. 3

    b. 5

    c. 7

    d. 9

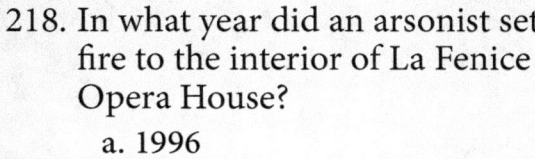
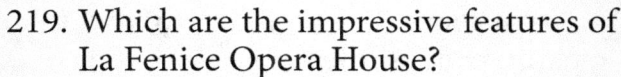

218. In what year did an arsonist set fire to the interior of La Fenice Opera House?
    a. 1996
    b. 1997
    c. 1998
    d. 1999

219. Which are the impressive features of La Fenice Opera House?
    a. Box seats of pastel blue with gold filigree
    b. Muses depicted on the ceiling
    c. A starburst chandelier
    d. All of the above

220. The Church of San Zaccaria contains which of the following?
    a. Bellini altarpiece
    b. Tintoretto painting
    c. Crypt of St. Zechariah, father of John the Baptist
    d. All of the above

221. San Giorgio Maggiore was designed by whom?
    a. Leon Battista Alberti
    b. Andrea Palladio
    c. Andrea Pozzo
    d. Donato Bramante

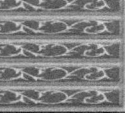

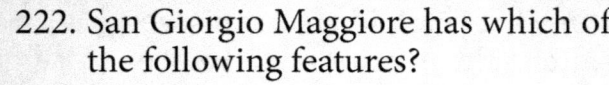

222. San Giorgio Maggiore has which of the following features?

    a. Tintoretto painting
    b. Bell tower
    c. Great views of Venice
    d. All of the above

223. The Accademia Gallery is Venice's top art museum. Which of the following painters does it feature?

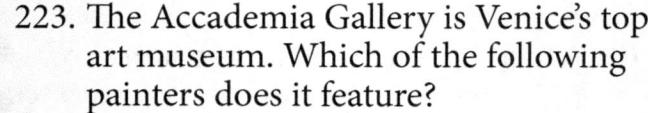

    a. Tiepolo
    b. Canaletto
    c. Giorgione
    d. All the above

224. The Accademia Gallery in Venice contains works by which of the following painters?

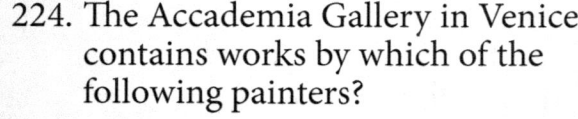

    a. Tiepolo
    b. Veronese
    c. Titian
    d. All of the above

225. The Accademia Gallery is located over which bridge?

    a. Costituzione
    b. Scaizi
    c. Accademia
    d. Rialto

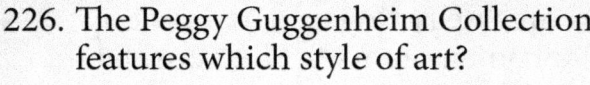

226. The Peggy Guggenheim Collection features which style of art?
 a. American Abstract Expressionism
 b. Surrealism
 c. Futurism
 d. All of the above

227. The Peggy Guggenheim Collection is one of Europe's best examples of art from which period?
 a. Early 19th century
 b. Late 19th century
 c. Early 20th century
 d. Late 20th century

228. Ca' Rezzonico gives a look at the rich and famous of Venice in which century?
 a. 15th
 b. 16th
 c. 17th
 d. 18th

229. Ca' Rezzonico contains paintings from which painter?
 a. Longhi
 b. Guardi
 c. Canaletto
 d. All the above

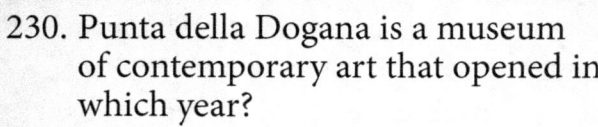

230. Punta della Dogana is a museum of contemporary art that opened in which year?
    a. 2008
    b. 2009
    c. 2010
    d. 2011

231. Punta della Dogana museum is housed in which former building?
    a. Bank of Venice
    b. Court House
    c. Customs house
    d. Napoleon's House

232. Ca' Pesaro International Gallery of Modern Art contains which of the following masterpieces?
    a. Chagall's Rabbi #2
    b. Klimt's Judith II
    c. Kandinsky's White Zig Zag
    d. All of the above

233. According to local authorities, Venice had how many visitors in 2019?
    a. 2.5 million
    b. 3.5 million
    c. 4.5 million
    d. 5.5 million

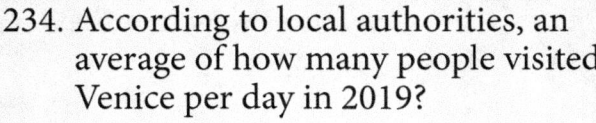

234. According to local authorities, an average of how many people visited Venice per day in 2019?
    a. 10,486
    b. 12,608
    c. 15,132
    d. 17,894

235. Palazzo Mocenigo is an example of how the wealthy lived in which century?
    a. 16th
    b. 17th
    c. 18th
    d. 19th

236. Palazzo Mocenigo shows life during Venice's Golden Age. Which are features of the house?
    a. Murano glass chandeliers
    b. Family portraits
    c. Ceiling paintings (c. 1790)
    d. All of the above

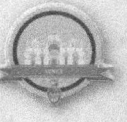

237. Frari Church is also known as what?
    a. Church of the Brothers
    b. Basilica di Santa María Gloriosa del Frari
    c. A Franciscan Church
    d. All of the above

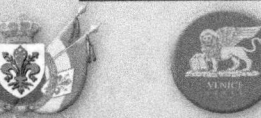

238. Frari Church features which of the following artists?

    a. Titian
    b. Giovanni Bellini
    c. Donatello
    d. All of the above

239. The word *ghetto* comes from the word meaning?

    a. Foundry
    b. Potters
    c. Small shops
    d. Island

240. The Arsenale is still a military base and closed to the public. The massive Arsenale gate is called?

    a. Pietro
    b. Porta Magna
    c. Tana
    d. Le Fari

241. How old is the residential neighborhood of Sant' Elena?

    a. 100 years old
    b. 115 years old
    c. 130 years old
    d. 145 years old

242. San Michele is the final resting place for Venetians and which of the following?
   a. Poet Ezra Pound
   b. Composer Igor Stravinsky
   c. Foreign VIP's
   d. All the above

243. Torcello church has a museum which contains which of the following?
   a. Manuscripts
   b. Roman sculpture
   c. Medieval sculpture
   d. All of the above

244. Palazzo Balbi was the palace of a 17th century captain general. That rank is equivalent to what military rank today?
   a. 3-star admiral
   b. 4-star admiral
   c. 5-star admiral
   d. 6-star admiral

245. The Palazzo Balbi flies how many flags?
   a. 1
   b. 2
   c. 3
   d. 4

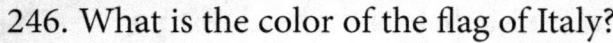

246. What is the color of the flag of Italy?
    a. Green
    b. White
    c. Red
    d. All of the above

247. What is on the European flag?
    a. Colors of red, white, and blue
    b. Blue with a ring of stars
    c. Colors of orange, white, and green
    d. Colors of blue and white

248. The lion on the flag of Venice has which colors?
    a. Red and gold
    b. Blue and yellow
    c. White and green
    d. Brown and yellow

249. At San Tomá, there is a fire station with boats ready to respond. What hides the boats?
    a. A tall wall of marble stolen from Athens
    b. Four arches
    c. A building jutting out
    d. A supporting structure holding up a bridge

250. What is the name of the main building at the University of Venice?

    a. Ca' Foscari
    b. Ca' Rezzonico
    c. Ca' Rialto
    d. Accedemia

251. Palazzo Grassi was the last major palace built on the Grand Canal. When was it built?

    a. Early 1700s
    b. Mid 1700s
    c. Late 1700s
    d. Early 1800s

252. Palazzo Grassi was purchased by whom?

    a. An American tycoon
    b. A British monarch
    c. A French tycoon
    d. A German duke

253. The Accademia bridge was first constructed of steel in what year?

    a. 1854
    b. 1855
    c. 1856
    d. 1857

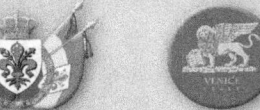

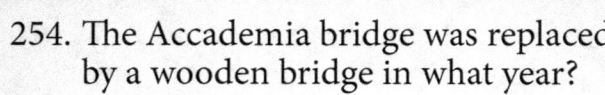

254. The Accademia bridge was replaced by a wooden bridge in what year?

    a. 1933
    b. 1934
    c. 1935
    d. 1936

255. What is one of the other names for La Salute Church?

    a. Scuola Dalmata
    b. Basílica di Santa Maria
    c. Church of St. Mary of Good Health
    d. San Giorgio

256. Palazzo Dario has which feature on the roof?

    a. Round chimneys
    b. Funnel-shaped chimneys
    c. Ship-shaped chimneys
    d. Cone-shaped chimneys

257. The Salviati Building once served as what?

    a. Justice court
    b. Warehouse for silks
    c. Glass Factory
    d. Warehouse for spices

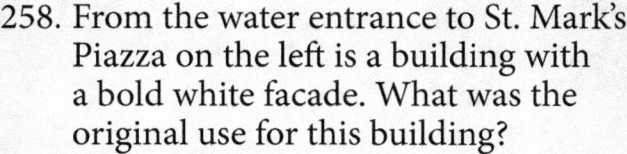

258. From the water entrance to St. Mark's Piazza on the left is a building with a bold white facade. What was the original use for this building?

    a. Offices for the doge
    b. The mint
    c. Apartments for visiting VIP's
    d. School of music

259. What was Venice's currency called when it was the Republic of Venice?

    a. Golden Lion
    b. Golden Ducat
    c. Golden Penny
    d. Golden Mark

260. Venice served as the middleman for trade from the east and the west, allowing them to profit from both sides. When did Venice reach its peak of wealth and power?

    a. 1450
    b. 1500
    c. 1550
    d. 1600

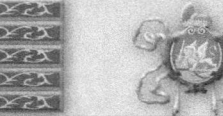

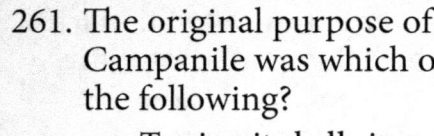

261. The original purpose of the
Campanile was which of
the following?

    a. To ring its bells in case of an
       emergency
    b. To impress visiting foreign VIP's
    c. To serve as an observation tower
    d. To ring its bells every 15 minutes

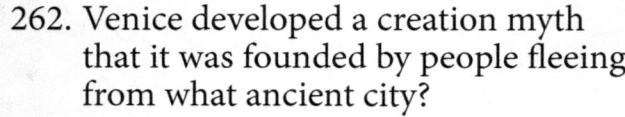

262. Venice developed a creation myth
that it was founded by people fleeing
from what ancient city?

    a. Cairo
    b. Alexandria
    c. Athens
    d. Troy

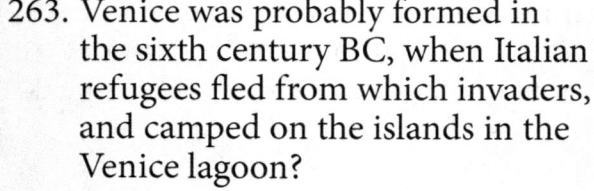

263. Venice was probably formed in
the sixth century BC, when Italian
refugees fled from which invaders,
and camped on the islands in the
Venice lagoon?

    a. Ottomans
    b. Lombards
    c. Greeks
    d. Byzantines

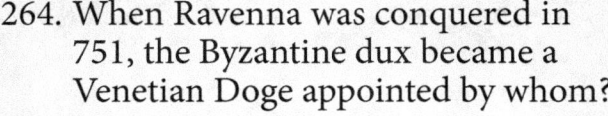

264. When Ravenna was conquered in 751, the Byzantine dux became a Venetian Doge appointed by whom?

    a. Merchant families
    b. The Pope
    c. The Roman emperor
    d. The Citizens of Venice

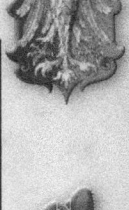

265. In 992, Venice earned special trading rights with the Byzantine empire in return for accepting which sovereignty?

    a. Roman
    b. Byzantine
    c. Greek
    d. Vatican

266. Venice grew richer and gained independence in what year?

    a. 992
    b. 1026
    c. 1082
    d. 1104

267. Venice retained trading advantages with the Byzantine Empire by offering it the use of what?

    a. The Venetian Army
    b. The Venetian Navy
    c. The right to borrow money
    d. A percentage of the trading profits

268. In what year was Venice first called a commune?
   a. 1046
   b. 1078
   c. 1092
   d. 1144

269. By the twelfth century, Venice and the remainder of which Empire engaged in a series of trade wars?
   a. Roman
   b. Byzantine
   c. Greek
   d. Ottoman

270. In which century did Venice agree to transport a crusade to the Holy Land?
   a. Early 13th
   b. Mid 13th
   c. Late 13th
   d. Early 14th

271. When the Crusaders couldn't pay Venice for passage, who promised to pay Venice?
   a. The Pope
   b. The Roman emperor
   c. The heir of a deposed Byzantine emperor
   d. Great Britain

272. The Crusaders sieged, captured, and sacked what city and moved the treasures to Venice?

    a. Athens

    b. Constantinople

    c. Alexandria

    d. Cairo

273. In which century did Venetian expansion target the Italian mainland with the capture of Vicenza, Verona, Padua, and Udine?

    a. 12th

    b. 13th

    c. 14th

    d. 15th

274. The construction of the Basilica of St. Anthony started immediately after St. Anthony's death in what year?

    a. 1231

    b. 1245

    c. 1264

    d. 1287

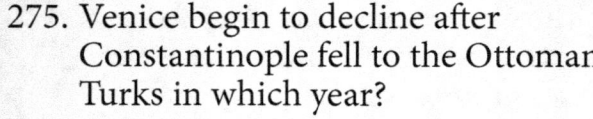

275. Venice begin to decline after Constantinople fell to the Ottoman Turks in which year?

    a. 1453
    b. 1457
    c. 1463
    d. 1466

276. Venice's decline occurred after Portuguese sailors had rounded Africa, opening another trading route to where?

    a. Europe
    b. Asia
    c. South Africa
    d. North Africa

277. There are two columns at the entrance to St. Mark's Piazza. Which is atop one of them?

    a. St. Theodore
    b. A sword
    c. A fish
    d. An arrow

278. Who organized the League of Cambrai to challenge Venice, defeating the city?

a. The Pope
b. The Roman emperor
c. Constantine
d. The Ottoman emperor

279. Venice did not halt its decline, even after winning the Battle of Lepanto over the Turks in which year?

a. 1565
b. 1568
c. 1571
d. 1574

280. When did the Pope Paul V place Venice under a papal interdict for, amongst other things, trying priests in a secular court?

a. 1606
b. 1608
c. 1609
d. 1611

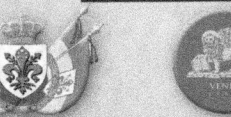

281. Venice declined as which other maritime powers secured Atlantic and African trade routes?

    a. The British
    b. The Dutch
    c. Both a and b
    d. Neither a nor b

282. The Venetian Republic came to an end in what year, after Napoleon's French army forced the city to agree to a new, pro-French, "democratic" government?

    a. 1795
    b. 1797
    c. 1799
    d. 1801

283. Venice was briefly which of the following after a peace treaty with Napoleon?

    a. Austrian
    b. British
    c. French
    d. German

284. Venice became French after the Battle of Austerlitz in what year?
    a. 1803
    b. 1804
    c. 1805
    d. 1806

285. After the fall of Napoleon from power, Venice was placed again under what country's rule?
    a. Austria
    b. Germany
    c. Spain
    d. Britain

286. The further decline of Venice set in when it was linked to the mainland for the first time by a railway in what year?
    a. 1843
    b. 1844
    c. 1845
    d. 1846

287. When did the number of tourists begin to exceed the local population in Venice?
    a. 1845
    b. 1846
    c. 1847
    d. 1848

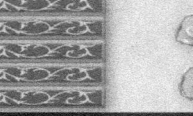

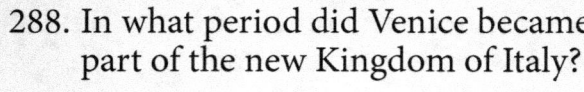

288. In what period did Venice became part of the new Kingdom of Italy?

    a. 1840s
    b. 1850s
    c. 1860s
    d. 1870s

289. The majority of the beautiful buildings in Venice are constructed on a base of what?

    a. Platforms of petrified wood
    b. Concrete pilings
    c. Steel pilings
    d. Granite blocks

290. In Venice there are about how many chimneys?

    a. 5,000
    b. 6,000
    c. 7,000
    d. 8,000

291. How many different types and shapes of chimneys are there in Venice?

    a. 10
    b. 12
    c. 15
    d. 18

292. How many bell towers are there in Venice?
   a. 132
   b. 156
   c. 170
   d. 189

293. The Campanile in St. Mark's Piazza is Italy's_____ tallest bell tower,
   a. 3rd
   b. 4th
   c. 5th
   d. 6th

294. In the year 402, where did the settlers cut down trees and take them to Venice?
   a. Slovenia
   b. Croatia
   c. Montenegro
   d. All the above

295. Houses in Venice are numbered according to what?
   a. Streets
   b. Districts
   c. Wards
   d. Precincts

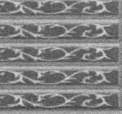

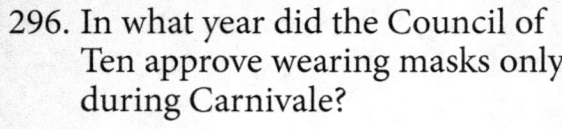

296. In what year did the Council of Ten approve wearing masks only during Carnivale?

    a. 1608
    b. 1609
    c. 1610
    d. 1611

297. The first public casino in the world was opened in Venice in which year?

    a. 1625
    b. 1627
    c. 1632
    d. 1638

298. Some experts believe Venice could be a ghost town by what year, with only tourists visiting by day?

    a. 2525
    b. 2030
    c. 2035
    d. 2040

299. Venice is sinking at the rate of how many millimeters a year?

    a. 1 – 2
    b. 2 - 3
    c. 3 - 4
    d. 4 - 5

300. The first woman in the world to graduate with a degree in theology, was born in Venice in what year?
    a. 1599
    b. 1624
    c. 1646
    d. 1687

301. The early settlers of Venice cut down trees to make 1,106,657 wooden stakes. How long were the stakes?
    a. 10 feet
    b. 13 feet
    c. 16 feet
    d. 19 feet

302. The total process from cutting the trees to building platforms for buildings to rest on took about how long?
    a. 2 years
    b. 3 years
    c. 4 years
    d. 5 years

303. Venice was listed as a World Heritage Site by the UNESCO in what year?
    a. 1985
    b. 1987
    c. 1991
    d. 1994

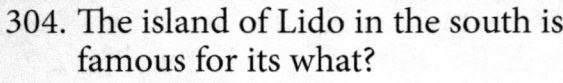

304. The island of Lido in the south is famous for its what?

    a. Lacemaking
    b. Long sandy beach
    c. Glass blowing
    d. Jewish community

305. How many bridges in Venice are made of stone?

    a. 100
    b. 200
    c. 300
    d. 400

306. About how many bridges in Venice are made of iron?

    a. 50
    b. 60
    c. 70
    d. 80

307. About how many bridges in Venice are made of wood?

    a. 20
    b. 30
    c. 40
    d. 50

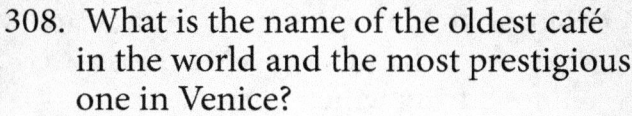

308. What is the name of the oldest café in the world and the most prestigious one in Venice?

    a. Gran Caffè Quadri
    b. Caffè Florian
    c. Caffè Aurora
    d. Gran Caffè Chioggia

309. In what year was the oldest cafe in Venice and the world opened?

    a. 1690
    b. 1705
    c. 1720
    d. 1730

310. The price in 2021 of two coffees at the world's and Venice's oldest cafe was about how much?

    a. 10 euros
    b. 15 euros
    c. 20 euros
    d. 25 euros

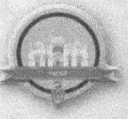

311. The Republic of Venice was also called what?

    a. La Serenissima
    b. La Dominante
    c. Queen of the Adriatic
    d. All of the above

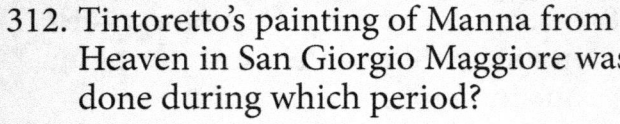

312. Tintoretto's painting of Manna from Heaven in San Giorgio Maggiore was done during which period?

    a. 1590 – 1591
    b. 1591 – 1592
    c. 1592 – 1593
    d. 1593 – 1594

313. The Casino di Venezia was originally known as what?

    a. Customs House
    b. Home of sea captains
    c. Ca' Vendramin Calergi
    d. None of the above

314. The Casino di Venezia later became a house for the Italian royalty and a vacation home for which famous composer?

    a. Richard Wagner
    b. Girolamo Abos
    c. Agostino Accorimboni
    d. Andrew Adolfati

315. In what year did the city of Venice purchase the former casino building?

    a. 1928
    b. 1967
    c. 1946
    d. 1956

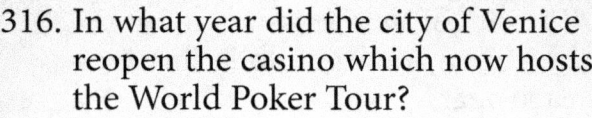

316. In what year did the city of Venice reopen the casino which now hosts the World Poker Tour?

    a. 1956
    b. 1959
    c. 1972
    d. 1978

317. In the past, being a Venice gondolier was a profession that was passed from father to son. What do you need today to be a gondolier?

    a. A professional License
    b. Pass an exam
    c. Purchase a license from a retiring gondolier
    d. All of the above

318. To become a fully licensed gondolier, applicants have to buy the license of a dead or retiring gondolier for about how much?

    a. Five hundred thousand
    b. Multiple six figures
    c. One million six hundred thousand
    d. Two million

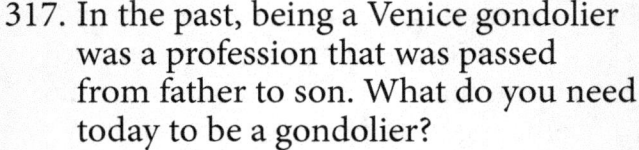
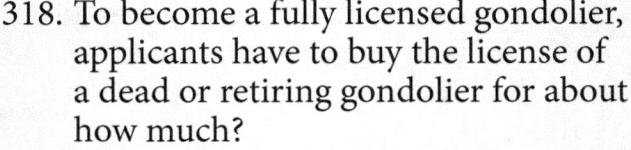

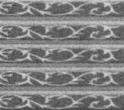

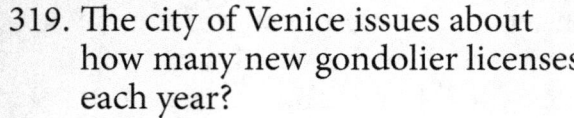

319. The city of Venice issues about how many new gondolier licenses each year?

    a. 1
    b. 2
    c. 3
    d. 4

320. The job of gondolier is historically a man's job. Today, there is a female gondolier. Giorgia Boscolo is the first female gondolier in Venice. When did she get her license?

    a. August 2010
    b. October 2010
    c. December 2010
    d. April 2011

321. A special law in Venice requires all gondolas to be black. The law was passed by the Venice Senate on what date?

    a. July 21, 1547
    b. January 7, 1553
    c. April 19, 1559
    d. October 8. 1562

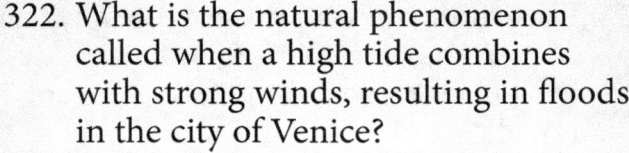

322. What is the natural phenomenon called when a high tide combines with strong winds, resulting in floods in the city of Venice?

    a. Temporale violento
    b. Acque alta
    c. Forte tifone
    d. Fuoco bruciante

323. The highest flood recorded in Venice happened on November 4, 1About what percentage of shops, businesses, and studios were damaged or destroyed?

    a. 25
    b. 50
    c. 75
    d. 90

324. The second highest flood in Venice occurred on November 12, 2 About what percentage of Venice was flooded?

    a. 70%
    b. 80%
    c. 90%
    d. 95%

325. Boat rides and walking are the only two means of transportation allowed in Venice. Which of the following are not allowed?

    a. Bicycles
    b. Skateboards
    c. Roller skates
    d. All of the above

326. Venice has over how many palaces?

    a. 187
    b. 213
    c. 237
    d. 285

327. The Calle Varisco is one of the narrowest streets in the world and the narrowest street in the Venice. How wide is it at its narrowest point?

    a. 53 cm
    b. 87 cm
    c. 91 cm
    d. 99 cm

328. Venice was founded by Roman refugees fleeing from whom in the 5th century?

    a. Roman soldiers
    b. Huns and Germanic tribes
    c. Ottoman Turks
    d. Persians

329. The official founding of the city of Venice is identified on which date with the inauguration of the San Giacomo church?

    a. January 25, 421
    b. February 25, 421
    c. March 25, 421
    d. April 25, 421

330. The Venice Carnival is world famous for its elegant masks. It started in what year as a celebration of a Venetian military victory?

    a. 1148
    b. 1156
    c. 1162
    d. 1171

331. The Venice Carnival rose in popularity in which century?

    a. 16th
    b. 17th
    c. 18th
    d. 19th

332. In what year was the Venice Carnival made illegal by Austria?

    a. 1789
    b. 1797
    c. 1801
    d. 1807

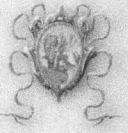

333. The Italian government restored the Venice Carnival in what year?

    a. 1971
    b. 1979
    c. 1985
    d. 1988

334. *Ciao*, an Italian word meaning hello and goodbye, is now used frequently in many languages around the world. The word originally comes from Venice: *s-ciào vostro*, which literally means what?

    a. "Happy to see you"
    b. "See you later"
    c. "Until next time"
    d. "I am your slave"

335. According to local tradition, if a couple in a gondola kiss when passing under a bridge, what will happen?

    a. They will remain in love forever.
    b. They will separate.
    c. They will divorce.
    d. They will have many children.

336. Marco Polo was born in Venice. He died at the age of 70 in Venice on what date?

    a. October 18, 1323
    b. December 11, 1323
    c. January 8, 1324
    d. July 14, 1324

337. The Ca' Dario, or Palazzo Dario, located on the Grand Canal in Venice is known as the Cursed Palace, mainly due to its dark history. It's said that whoever would stay in the palace would either die or go bankrupt. In 2002, who died when renting the Ca' Dario.

    a. John Entwistle
    b. Bob Dylan
    c. Connie Francis
    d. Dwayne Williams

338. Which famous movie was filmed in Venice?

    a. *Lara Croft: Tomb Raider*
    b. *Indiana Jones and the Last Crusade*
    c. James Bond - *Moonraker*
    d. All the above

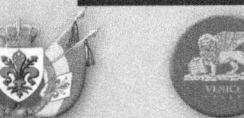

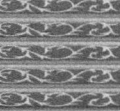

339. In what year was Constantinople attacked and artisans in glass fled to Venice?

    a. 1198
    b. 1202
    c. 1204
    d. 1206

340. Music composer Antonio Vivaldi was born in Venice in what year?

    a. 1672
    b. 1678
    c. 1681
    d. 1685

341. About how many hidden gardens are there is Venice?

    a. 200
    b. 300
    c. 400
    d. 500

342. 342.In relation to Rome, where is Venice located?

    a. North
    b. East
    c. South
    d. West

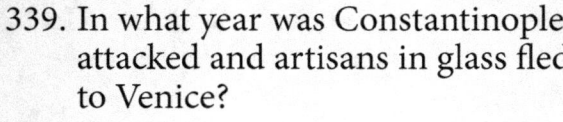

343. In Venice, what is a name that is especially approved for baby boys?
    a. Raman
    b. Turk
    c. Venice
    d. None of the above

344. What is the lucky number for the name Venice?
    a. 1
    b. 2
    c. 3
    d. 4

345. In 453 AD, which famous warrior invaded Italy?
    a. Hannibal
    b. Attila the Hun
    c. Arminius
    d. Boudica

346. Celtic people called the Veneti lived in what is now northeast Italy. When did they become Roman citizens?
    a. 72 to 21 BC
    b. 90 to 27 BC
    c. 82 to 31 BC
    d. 88 to 24 BC

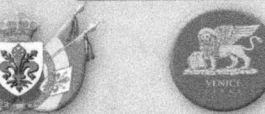

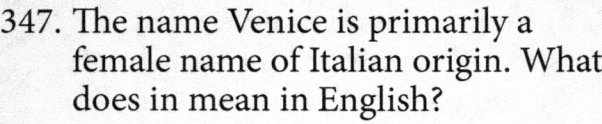

347. The name Venice is primarily a female name of Italian origin. What does in mean in English?
    a. The duchess
    b. The maiden
    c. Name of an Italian city
    d. Difficult to invade

348. How many people were named Venice in 2020 in California?
    a. 3,315
    b. 3,697
    c. 3,871
    d. 3,943

349. In which state is the name Venice the most popular?
    a. New York
    b. Pennsylvania
    c. California
    d. Florida

350. What percentage of people in California in 2020 were named Venice?
    a. 0.001%
    b. 0.007%
    c. 0.011%
    d. 0.018%

351. What does the Italian phrase *per favore* mean?

    a. You're welcome
    b. Please
    c. Excuse me
    d. Cheers

352. What does the Italian word *grazie* mean?

    a. Please
    b. Thank you
    c. Cheers
    d. Excuse me

353. What does the Italian word *scusi* mean?

    a. To your health
    b. Excuse me (for attention)
    c. Thank you
    d. Please

354. Venice's many lions express which of the following moods:

    a. Sadness that a favorite son has died
    b. Triumphant after a naval victory
    c. Smiling at a soccer team victory
    d. All of the above

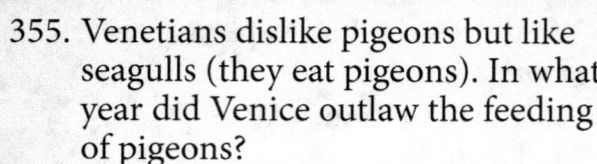

355. Venetians dislike pigeons but like seagulls (they eat pigeons). In what year did Venice outlaw the feeding of pigeons?

    a. 2007
    b. 2008
    c. 2009
    d. 2010

356. The first coffeehouse was opened in Venice in which century?

    a. 15th
    b. 16th
    c. 17th
    d. 18th

357. By what year were dozens of cafes operating in St. Mark's Piazza?

    a. 1675
    b. 1700
    c. 1725
    d. 1750

358. By what year were about 200 cafes operating in Venice?

    a. 1675
    b. 1700
    c. 1725
    d. 1750

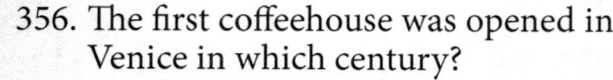
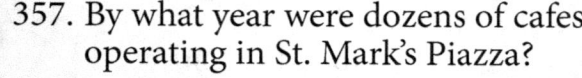

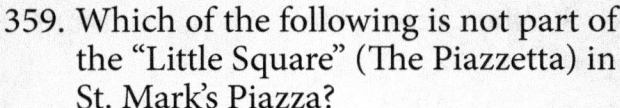

359. Which of the following is not part of the "Little Square" (The Piazzetta) in St. Mark's Piazza?

 a. The clock tower
 b. The Doges Palace
 c. The library
 d. The lagoon

360. Café Florian (in St. Mark's Piazza) has been a popular spot for a discreet rendezvous since what year?

 a. 1680
 b. 1700
 c. 1720
 d. 1740

361. The Doge's Palace has gothic arches with a Venetian flair, a trefoil or a quatrefoil. What are these?

 a. Box-like pieces that are cut out
 b. Round pieces that are cut out
 c. Triangular pieces that are cut out
 d. Three-leaf and four-leaf clovers

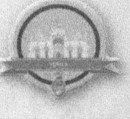

362. At the lagoon entrance to St. Mark's Piazza is a column with St. Theodore battling what?

 a. Atilla the Hun
 b. A crocodile
 c. Ottoman Turks
 d. A dragoon

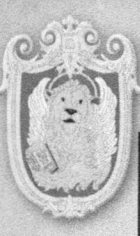

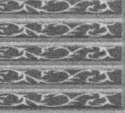

363. St. Mark replaced which patron saint of Venice?

    a. St. Francis
    b. St. Stephen
    c. St. Philip
    d. St. Theodore

364. The two columns at the lagoon entrance to St. Mark's Piazza were used for what?

    a. To show the wealth of Venice
    b. To show that Venice could take anything it wanted
    c. For public executions
    d. For flags that to be strung between them

365. What is the name of the small park near St. Mark's Piazza?

    a. Sotoportego
    b. Cavalletto
    c. San Giorgio
    d. Giardinetti Reali

366. What is the name of the lace shop housed in a decommissioned chapel near the northwest corner of St. Mark's Piazza?

    a. Florian
    b. Il Merletto
    c. Tetarchs
    d. Medardo

367. The Venetian Lagoon is how many feet below sea level at its deepest point?

    a. 97
    b. 109
    c. 137
    d. 164

368. When viewed from above Venice is shaped like what?

    a. Carrot
    b. Potato
    c. Fish
    d. Snake

369. The price of a gondola ride in Venice is always the same for all 425 gondoliers, no more and no less. This is the decree of the _____?

    a. The Doge
    b. Gondoliers' Association
    c. Venice city council
    d. Italian government

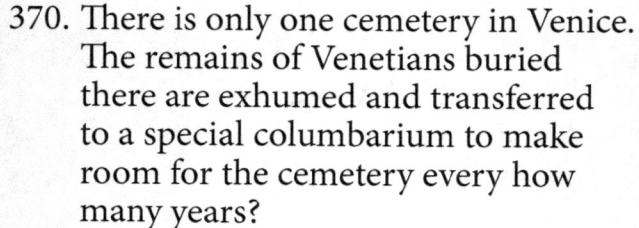

370. There is only one cemetery in Venice. The remains of Venetians buried there are exhumed and transferred to a special columbarium to make room for the cemetery every how many years?

    a. 7
    b. 9
    c. 11
    d. 13

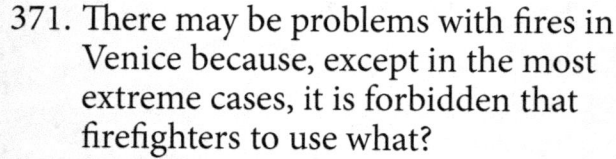

371. There may be problems with fires in Venice because, except in the most extreme cases, it is forbidden that firefighters to use what?

    a. Fire extinguishers
    b. City water
    c. Seawater
    d. None of the above

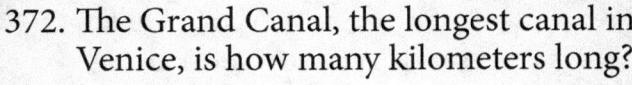

372. The Grand Canal, the longest canal in Venice, is how many kilometers long?

    a. Four kilometers
    b. Five kilometers
    c. Six kilometers
    d. Seven kilometers

373. Venice was the main maritime power of the Mediterranean between which centuries?

    a. 12th - 14th
    b. 13th - 15th
    c. 14th – 16th
    d. 15th - 17th

374. The oldest bridges do not have stairs, as people traveled on horseback until which century?

    a. 14
    b. 15
    c. 16th
    d. 17

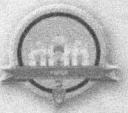

375. Which of the following are strictly prohibited in Venice? The exception is made only for children.

    a. Bicycles
    b. Cars
    c. Dogs
    d. Speedboats

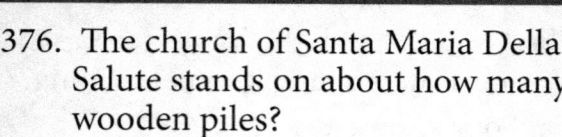

376. The church of Santa Maria Della Salute stands on about how many wooden piles?

    a. Twenty-five thousand
    b. Fifty thousand
    c. Seventy-five thousand
    d. One hundred thousand

377. In its history, Venice has been rebuilt how many times?

    a. Two
    b. Three
    c. Four
    d. Five

378. Venice is a city in which part of Italy?

    a. Southeast
    b. Northeast
    c. Southwest
    d. Northwest

379. The area of Venice is believed to have been inhabited since the ___ century BC?

    a. 8th
    b. 9th
    c. 10th
    d. 11th

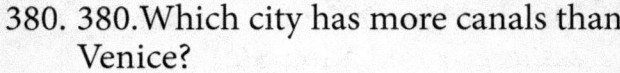

380. 380.Which city has more canals than Venice?

    a. Amsterdam
    b. London
    c. Brussels
    d. Rotterdam

381. Which German city has more canals than Venice and Amsterdam together?

    a. Frankfurt
    b. Berlin
    c. Hamburg
    d. None of the above

382. If you take the bus in Venice, what kind will it be?

    a. Water
    b. Diesel
    c. Electric
    d. Gas

383. Which of the following are districts in Venice?

    a. San Polo
    b. Castello
    c. Dorsoduro
    d. All the above

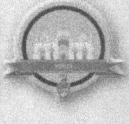

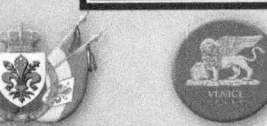

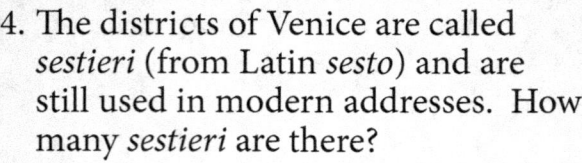

384. The districts of Venice are called *sestieri* (from Latin *sesto*) and are still used in modern addresses. How many *sestieri* are there?
   a. Five
   b. Six
   c. Seven
   d. Eight

385. The first woman to ever graduate from a university was from Venice. Her name was Elena Lucrezia Cornaro Piscopia. She graduated on June 25, 1678 from what university?
   a. The University of Padua
   b. The University of Rome
   c. The University of Naples
   d. The University of Venice

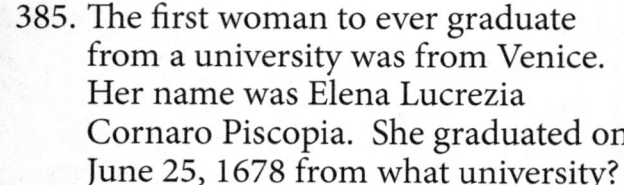

386. What are the best things to buy in Venice?
   a. Lace
   b. Glass
   c. Both a and b
   d. Neither a nor b

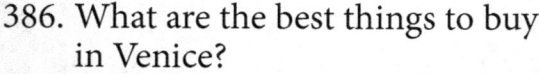

387. Some houses in Venice are larger at the top than at the bottom and windows often stick out onto the road. What is this peculiar architectural feature called?

    a. Perla
    b. Bello
    c. Barbacani
    d. Forte

388. How many bells are in St. Mark's tower?

    a. 3
    b. 4
    c. 5
    d. 6

389. The gondola is a narrow, black, pointed boat. It has a metal piece at he bow that is called a _____?

    a. Ferro
    b. Forte
    c. Bello
    d. Perla

390. Which applies to the word "Doge?"

    a. Top ruler of Venice
    b. First elected in 697 AD
    c. Ludovico Manin was the last
    d. All of the the above

391. The top of a gondola's *ferro* represents the Doge's hat, the six forward prongs symbolize the six *sestieri*. What does the 7th prong, which points backwards, represent?

    a. St. Mark's Basilica
    b. Giudecca Island
    c. The Doge's Palace
    d. San Giorgio Church

392. The Republic of Venice lasted over 1000 years and was comprised of territories as far away as_____?

    a. Dalmatia
    b. Cyprus
    c. Turkey
    d. All of the above

393. Which city was the arch enemy of Venice? (Hint: It was another important maritime power, which Venice fought for many years over the control of the trading routes.)

    a. Genoa
    b. Rome
    c. Florence
    d. Naples

394. If you look at the map of Venice, you may see that the Grand Canal resembles which of the following?

    a. A whale
    b. A rat
    c. A snake
    d. A fish

395. Venice only has one piazza, St. Mark's Piazza. What are all the other 'squares' called?

    a. Sestieri
    b. San Polo
    c. Campo
    d. Dorsoduro

396. What is the Venetian word for "street"?

    a. Fondamenta
    b. Calle
    c. Piscina
    d. All of the above

397. In some Venetian paintings the lion carries a sword. This usually means the paintings date back to a time when Venice was in what status?

    a. At peace
    b. At war
    c. In negotiations
    d. Doesn't mean anything. It' just a painting.

398. Which of the following is true of the Doge?

    a. He was the head of state in Venice.
    b. He ruled for life.
    c. He did not rule by divine right.
    d. All of the above

399. On which sea is Venice?

    a. The Ionian Sea
    b. The Tyrrhenian
    c. The Aegean
    d. The Adriatic

400. Which of the following is true of the Doge Palace?

    a. It was the home of the Doge.
    b. It was the seat of the republic.
    c. It contains the grand council rooms.
    d. All of the above

401. In what year did Venetians ask the emperor in Constantinople to protect them from the marauding Franks?
  a. 808
  b. 810
  c. 812
  d. 814

402. In the 10th century how many Venetians merchants lived and worked in Constantinople?
  a. 5,000
  b. 7,500
  c. 10,000
  d. 12,500

403. In what year did the Byzantine emperor expel Venetian merchants from Constantinople?
  a. 1171
  b. 1175
  c. 1181
  d. 1187

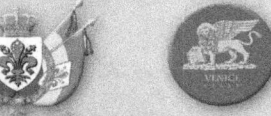

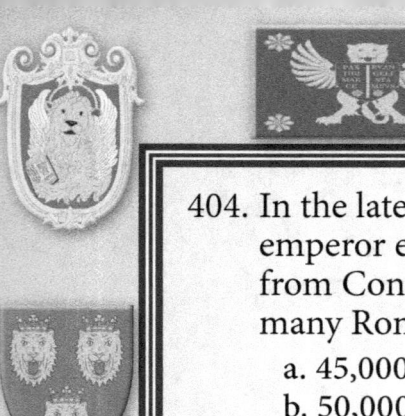
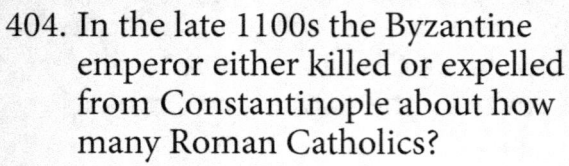

404. In the late 1100s the Byzantine emperor either killed or expelled from Constantinople about how many Roman Catholics?
    a. 45,000
    b. 50,000
    c. 55,000
    d. 60,000

405. Venice made her ships available to the Pope to transport Crusaders to save the Holy Land from the Muslims. Led by the Doge, where did they end up?
    a. Jerusalem
    b. Athens
    c. Constantinople
    d. Antloch

406. Venice transported more than how many Crusaders?
    a. 20,000
    b. 30,000
    c. 40,000
    d. 50,000

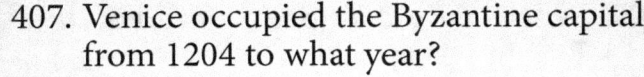

407. Venice occupied the Byzantine capital from 1204 to what year?

    a. 1255
    b. 1257
    c. 1259
    d. 1261

408. During the occupation of the Byzantine capital, ships returning to Venice from there were required to do what?

    a. Pay the port charges in gold
    b. Bring a souvenir
    c. Carry Venetian citizens free of charge
    d. Bring 10 slaves to the Doge

409. Venice transported crusaders in which Crusade?

    a. Second Crusade
    b. Third Crusade
    c. Fourth Crusade
    d. Fifth Crusade

410. The economy of Venice rose after the Fourth Crusade. What happened to the Byzantine Empire's economy?

    a. It also rose.
    b. It faded.
    c. It stayed the same.
    d. It went up and down.

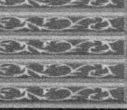

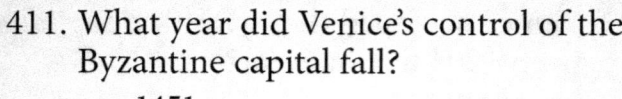

411. What year did Venice's control of the Byzantine capital fall?

    a. 1451
    b. 1452
    c. 1453
    d. 1454

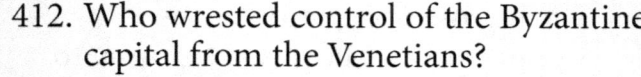

412. Who wrested control of the Byzantine capital from the Venetians?

    a. The Turks
    b. The Ottomans
    c. The Huns
    d. The Romans

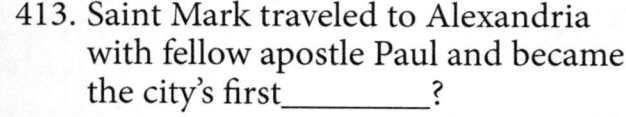

413. Saint Mark traveled to Alexandria with fellow apostle Paul and became the city's first_____?

    a. Priest
    b. Lecturer
    c. Bishop
    d. Cardinal

414. Which of the following is a nickname for the Doge's Palace?

    a. "The Wedding Cake"
    b. "The Tablecloth"
    c. "The Pink House"
    d. All of the above

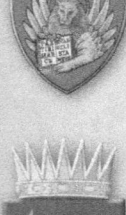

415. Doge's Palace is unfortified and has no city walls. It was the Doge's way of saying which of the following?

    a. "I am elected."
    b. "I am loved."
    c. "I do not fear my own people."
    d. All of the above

416. The Doge's Palace was originally built in which period?

    a. 600s
    b. 700s
    c. 800s
    d. 900s

417. Most of what we see today at Doge's Palace was added after what years?

    a. 1000s
    b. 1100s
    c. 1200s
    d. 1300s

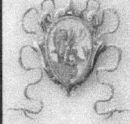
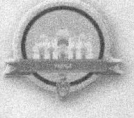

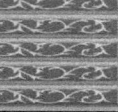

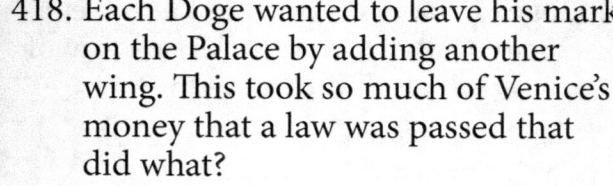

418. Each Doge wanted to leave his mark on the Palace by adding another wing. This took so much of Venice's money that a law was passed that did what?

    a. Levied an enormous fine for anyone suggesting a new building

    b. Making every sea captain contribute half his wealth to the city

    c. Charged an enormous tax on every merchant ship entering Venice

    d. All of the above

419. Foreign dignitaries on business with the Doge had to do which of the following?

    a. Ascend the Golden Staircase

    b. Ascend the Stairway of Giants

    c. Kneel to the Doge

    d. Swear allegiance to the Doge

420. What is at the top of the Stairway of Giants?

    a. Two nearly nude male statues

    b. Two horses standing on top of a white column

    c. Two giant vases

    d. A fountain on each side with a nude female

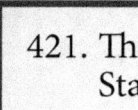

421. The Doge would only descend the Stairway of Giants for whom?

    a. The Emperor
    b. The King
    c. The Pope
    d. No one

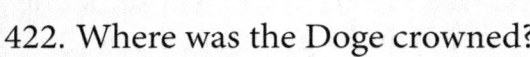

422. Where was the Doge crowned?

    a. In the Hall of Justice
    b. Atop the Golden Staircase
    c. Atop the Stairway of Giants
    d. At St. Mark's Basilica

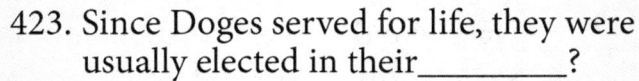

423. Since Doges served for life, they were usually elected in their_____?

    a. 50s
    b. 60s
    c. 70s
    d. 80s

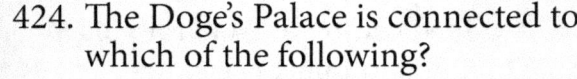

424. The Doge's Palace is connected to which of the following?

    a. Frari Church
    b. San Zaccaria
    c. St. Mark's Basilica
    d. San Sabastiano

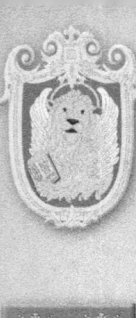

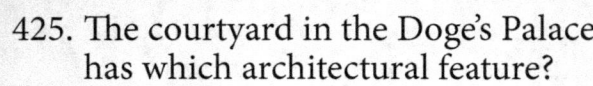

425. The courtyard in the Doge's Palace has which architectural feature?

    a. Renaissance arches
    b. Baroque awnings
    c. Gothic spires
    d. All of the above

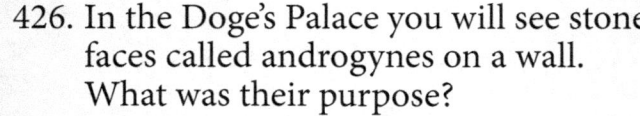

426. In the Doge's Palace you will see stone faces called androgynes on a wall. What was their purpose?

    a. Anyone with a complaint could drop a slip of paper into the androgyne's mouth.
    b. Anyone with a suspicion could accuse someone by putting a slip of paper into the androgyne's mouth.
    c. Anyone with gossip could put it on slip of paper and into the androgyne's mouth.
    d. All of the above

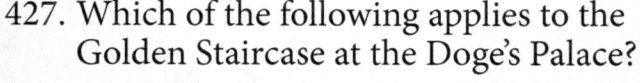

427. Which of the following applies to the Golden Staircase at the Doge's Palace?

    a. A gilded ceiling of 24 karat gold
    b. Designed to impress visitors
    c. Architectural propaganda
    d. All of the above

428. To be elected, the Doge had to meet which of the following requirements.
    a. He and his family had to move into the Palace.
    b. He couldn't open official mail in private.
    c. He couldn't leave the Palace unescorted.
    d. All of the above

429. The Doge and his family lived in more than how many rooms at the Palace?
    a. 10
    b. 11
    c. 12
    d. 13

430. Which of the following is to be found in the Doge's apartment?
    a. Gold coffered ceilings
    b. Walls filled with paintings
    c. A big stone fireplace
    d. All of the above

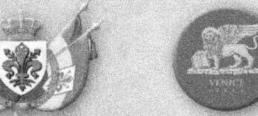

431. The Doge's Palace was decorated by only the finest Venetian painters. What happened to most of the paintings by Titian?

    a. They were sold to wealthy Europeans to fund expansion of the Palace.

    b. They were given to the Pope.

    c. They were destroyed in a fire.

    d. They were moved to the old office building.

432. The paintings in the Doge's Palace show the Venice of old. Which of the following is shown in the paintings of old Venice?

    a. The people of Venice

    b. Women showing off a major industry, such as textiles

    c. The cityscape

    d. All of the above

433. What can be said of the paintings by Veronese in Doge's Palace?

    a. Veronese used the best pigments.

    b. The painter used precious stones.

    c. The painter was a genius.

    d. All of the above

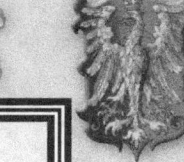
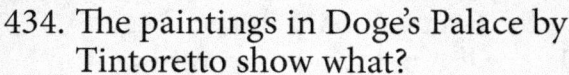

434. The paintings in Doge's Palace by Tintoretto show what?

    a. He didn't put his heart and soul into them.
    b. They were done by his workshop.
    c. He didn't use any precious materials.
    d. All of the above

435. Sala dello Scudo is the name of which room in the Doge's Palace?

    a. The Room of the Four Doors
    b. The Square Room
    c. The Shield Room
    d. All of the above

436. The Shield Room in the Doge's Palace is full of maps and globes. These maps can be used to trace the travels of Marco Polo to which country?

    a. Greece
    b. Palestine
    c. Arabia
    d. All of the above

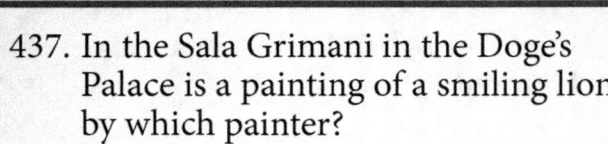

437. In the Sala Grimani in the Doge's Palace is a painting of a smiling lion by which painter?

    a. Titian
    b. Vittore Carpaccio
    c. Veronese
    d. Tintoretto

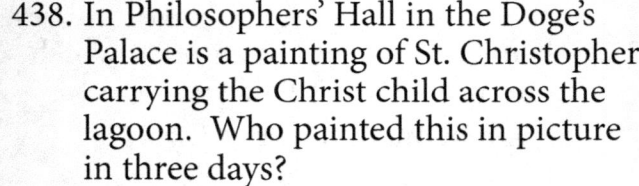

438. In Philosophers' Hall in the Doge's Palace is a painting of St. Christopher carrying the Christ child across the lagoon. Who painted this in picture in three days?

    a. Titian
    b. Vittore Carpaccio
    c. Veronese
    d. Tintoretto

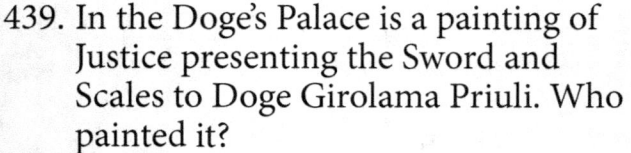

439. In the Doge's Palace is a painting of Justice presenting the Sword and Scales to Doge Girolama Priuli. Who painted it?

    a. Titian
    b. Veronese
    c. Jacopo Tintoretto
    d. None of the above

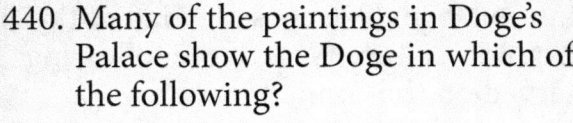

440. Many of the paintings in Doge's Palace show the Doge in which of the following?
    a. His one horned hat
    b. His robe of gold brocade
    c. His ermine cape
    d. All of the above

441. Sala delle Quattro Porte in the Doge's Palace was used to direct visitors to which of the following?
    a. The councils
    b. The courts
    c. The Doge
    d. All of the above

442. In St. Mark's Piazza are statues of water-bearing slaves. What function do they serve?
    a. Drain spouts
    b. Ornamentation
    c. Columns
    d. All of the above

443. In the 1400s, Venice had a reputation for which type of justice?
    a. Secret
    b. Harsh
    c. Swift
    d. All of the above

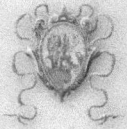
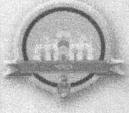

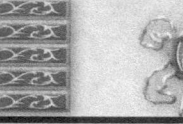

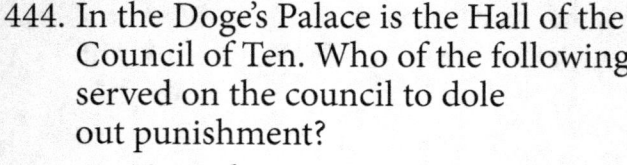

444. In the Doge's Palace is the Hall of the Council of Ten. Who of the following served on the council to dole out punishment?
   a. Ten judges
   b. The Doge
   c. Advisers to the Doge
   d. All of the above

445. The Council of Ten doled out punishment to whom?
   a. Murderers
   b. Traitors
   c. Moral violators
   d. All of the above

446. If you were accused by the Council of Ten, which of the following could happen?
   a. Thrown in jail
   b. Tortured
   c. Decapitated
   d. All of the above

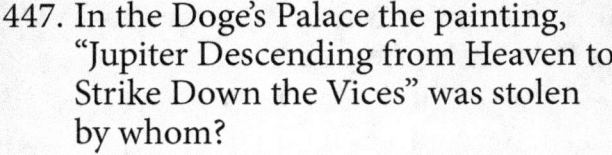

447. In the Doge's Palace the painting, "Jupiter Descending from Heaven to Strike Down the Vices" was stolen by whom?
 a. The last Doge
 b. The Pope
 c. Napoleon
 d. The Crusaders

448. In the Hall of the Council of Ten in the Doge's Palace is a secret door leading to the torture chamber or the prison. Which panel, to the right of center, is this door?
 a. Third
 b. Fourth
 c. Fifth
 d. Sixth

449. The Armory Museum in the Doge's Palace contains which of the following military items?
 a. Morions
 b. Falchions
 c. Ranseurs
 d. All of the above

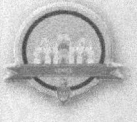

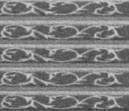

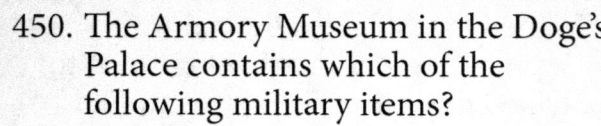

450. The Armory Museum in the Doge's Palace contains which of the following military items?

    a. Brigandines
    b. Targets
    c. Halberds
    d. All of the above

451. In the Armory Room in the Doge's Palace is an early 17th century machine gun. How many barrels does it have?

    a. 10
    b. 14
    c. 20
    d. 24

452. In the Armory Room in the Doge's Palace, the weapons to be used by the Council of Ten are marked with which of the following monograms?

    a. D-P
    b. C-X
    c. X-C
    d. P-D

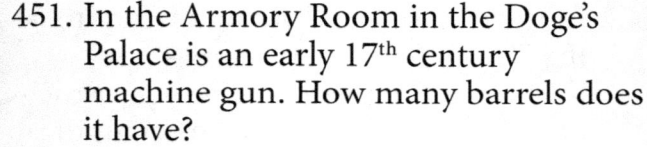

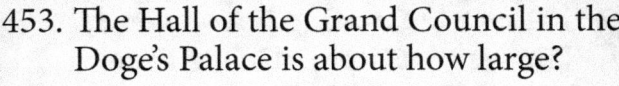

453. The Hall of the Grand Council in the Doge's Palace is about how large?

    a. 50 feet x 75 feet
    b. 100 feet x 125 feet
    c. 80 feet x 175 feet
    d. 100 feet x 175 feet

454. Which of the following were subordinate to the Grand Council?

    a. The Doge
    b. The Senate
    c. The Council of Ten
    d. All of the above

455. Which of the following were requirements to be on the Council of Nobles?

    a. Must be a wealthy man
    b. Must be over 25 years of age
    c. Must have a long bloodline
    d. All of the above

456. The painting by Tintoretto in the Hall of the Grand Council is how many square feet?

    a. 1,654
    b. 1,987
    c. 2,104
    d. 2,215

457. The largest painting in the world, by Tintoretto, is in the Doge's Palace. What is it called?

    a. Justice
    b. Peace
    c. Paradise
    d. Resurrection

458. In the Hall of the Grand Council in the Doge's Palace, the painting by Tintoretto depicts the top of heaven surrounded by how many people?

    a. 400
    b. 500
    c. 600
    d. 700

459. In the Hall of the Grand Council in the Doge's Palace are portraits of how many Doges?

    a. 52
    b. 68
    c. 76
    d. 81

460. Of the portraits of the Doge's one
is blacked, Doge Marin Falier. He
opposed the will of the Grand
Council in what year?

    a. 1328
    b. 1355
    c. 1373
    d. 1381

461. Doge Marin Faliero opposed the
will of the Grand Council. What
happened to him?

    a. He was tried for treason.
    b. He was beheaded.
    c. His portrait is covered with a
       black cloth.
    d. All of the above

462. In the Hall of the Grand Council is
an entire wall painted by Domenico.
Who was his father?

    a. Titian
    b. Veronese
    c. Giogoria
    d. Jacopo Tintoretto

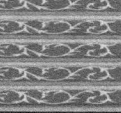

463. The entire wall painting along the right side of Paradise in the Hall of the Grand Council is entitled what?

    a. Triumph of Venice
    b. Siege of Constantinople
    c. Apotheosis of Venice
    d. Baccbus and Ariadne

464. The mighty wall of Constantinople repelled every attack for nearly how many years?

    a. 800
    b. 900
    c. 1000
    d. 1100

465. By about what year did Portugal break Venice's East-West trade monopoly?

    a. 1500
    b. 1525
    c. 1550
    d. 1575

466. In what year was the Battle of Lepanto, the last major victory for Venice's naval fleet?

    a. 1570
    b. 1571
    c. 1572
    d. 1573

467. The last Doge abdicated in what year?
    a. 1795
    b. 1796
    c. 1797
    d. 1798

468. The Doge's Palace had its own prison. Here the Doge could oversee which of the following punishments of his political opponents?
    a. Sentencing
    b. Torturing
    c. Jailing
    d. All the above

469. The prison at the Doge's Palace was filled with political prisoners by about when?
    a. 1400s
    b. 1500s
    c. 1600s
    d. 1700s

470. After the prison in the Doge's Palace was full, another prison was built across the canal. Which bridge connected them?
    a. Rialto
    b. Accademia
    c. Sighs
    d. Scalzi

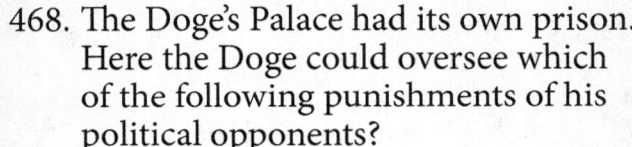

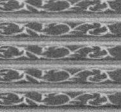

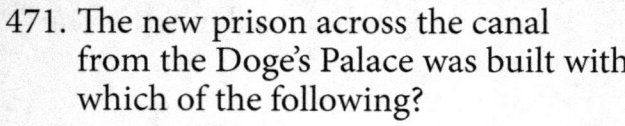

471. The new prison across the canal from the Doge's Palace was built with which of the following?

    a. Cold stone
    b. Wooden planks for beds
    c. A shelf for the prisoner
    d. All the above

472. Which Museum has a Doge's hat, paintings by the Bellini family, and statues by Canova?

    a. National Archaeological
    b. Accademia
    c. Correr
    d. Ca' Rezzonico

473. In the 1950s, which future Pope presided as patriarch and cardinal of Venice?

    a. Pope Pius XI
    b. Pope Paul VI
    c. Pope John Paul I
    d. Pope John XXIII

474. In the northwest corner of Campo San Zaccaria is a plaque listing all the things that were prohibited in what year?

    a. 1600
    b. 1610
    c. 1620
    d. 1630

475. The "Madonna and Child with Saints" was painted by Bellini in what year?

    a. 1495
    b. 1500
    c. 1505
    d. 1510

476. In the church of San Zaccaria is a painting, "Birth of John the Baptist." Who was the painter?

    a. Bellini
    b. Tintoretto
    c. Veronese
    d. Titian

477. How old was Bellini when he painted "Madonna and Child with Saints?"

    a. 60
    b. 65
    c. 70
    d. 75

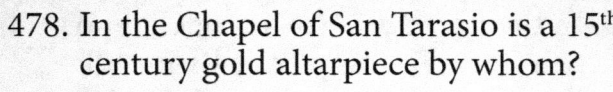

478. In the Chapel of San Tarasio is a 15th century gold altarpiece by whom?

    a. Antonio Vivarini
    b. Jacopo Amigoni
    c. Giovanni de Asola
    d. Pietro Liberi

479. By the waterfront near St. Mark's Piazza is an equestrian monument to Victor Emmanuel II. He became Italy's first king in what year?

    a. 1858
    b. 1859
    c. 1860
    d. 1861

480. On the night of July 25, 1755 Giacomo Casanova was arrested and imprisoned in the dreaded Piombi. When did he escape and reach Bolzano?

    a. September 18, 1755
    b. December 26, 1755
    c. August 30, 1756
    d. October 31, 1756

481. A single anonymous accusation was enough for Casanova to be arrested after a note was slipped into the Mouth of Secret Accusations in which room in the Doge's Palace?

    a. Senate Hall
    b. Hall of the Council of Ten
    c. Hall of the Compass
    d. Hall of the Grand Council

482. Casanova was a man with special gifts. Which of the following describes a gift of Casanova's?

    a. Legendary seducer
    b. Amateur scholar
    c. Actor
    d. All of the above

483. Casanova's memoir is entitled *The story of my escape from the Piombi.* In what year was it printed?

    a. 1756
    b. 1765
    c. 1788
    d. 1794

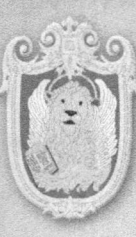

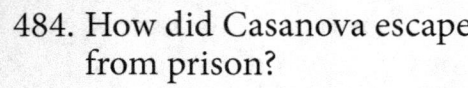

484. How did Casanova escape
from prison?

    a. By digging up wooden planks
    b. Climbed onto the roof
    c. Went through the attic
    d. All of the above

485. How did Casanova finally get free
from the Palace?

    a. By crossing the inside of the Palace
    b. Going down the Golden Staircase
    c. Being mistaken as a politician who
       had been locked in, so a guard let
       him out
    d. All of the above

486. Legend says that after escaping
from the prison he did which of
the following?

    a. Seduced the first lady he saw
    b. Stopped for coffee in San Marco
       square
    c. Checked into a hotel under an alias
    d. Went to a restaurant for a good
       meal

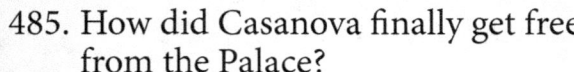
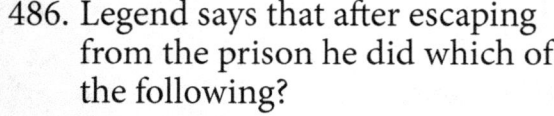

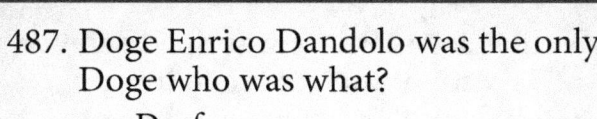

487. Doge Enrico Dandolo was the only Doge who was what?

   a. Deaf
   b. Totally disabled
   c. Blind
   d. Uneducated

488. There have been several fires at the Doge's Palace. On which of the following dates was there a major fire?

   a. 1483
   b. 1574
   c. 1577
   d. All of the above

489. The Venetian Republic fell in 1797 to the French. Which country followed in ruling Venice?

   a. Germany
   b. Austria
   c. Greece
   d. Portugal

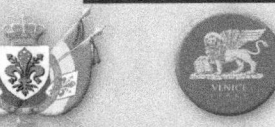

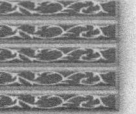

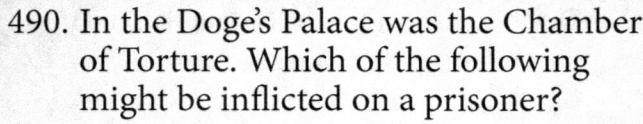

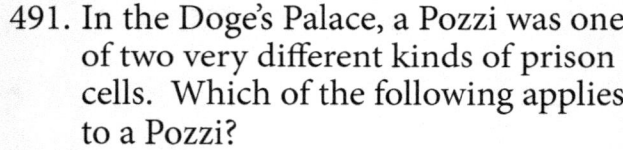

490. In the Doge's Palace was the Chamber of Torture. Which of the following might be inflicted on a prisoner?

    a. Waiting in complete darkness

    b. Hearing painful screams from other prisoners

    c. Being pulled by their arms with ropes

    d. All of the above

491. In the Doge's Palace, a Pozzi was one of two very different kinds of prison cells. Which of the following applies to a Pozzi?

    a. It's an Italian word meaning "wells."

    b. It's a place of detention.

    c. It's a little, wet cell with hardly any ventilation that reeks of human waste.

    d. All of the above

492. When a Doge moved into the Palace, what did he do for furniture?

    a. Purchased new with public funds

    b. Used furniture stolen from other countries

    c. Borrowed from friends, so his personal house would remain furnished

    d. Used his own personal furniture

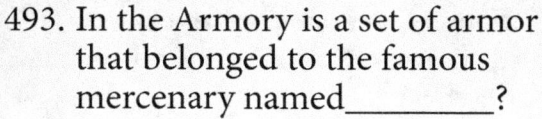

493. In the Armory is a set of armor that belonged to the famous mercenary named_____?
    a. Erasmo da Narni
    b. Carlo Goldeni
    c. Antonio Vivaldi
    d. Marco Polo

494. Ponte de Chiodo is one of only two bridges in Venice that are?
    a. Toll bridges
    b. Without parapets
    c. Have gardens on the bridge
    d. Are made of aluminum alloy

495. Scuola Grande di San Marco is a building dating back to 1What is it used for today?
    a. City hospital
    b. Museum of the History of Medicine
    c. To exhibit a collection of ancient books that line the walls
    d. All the above

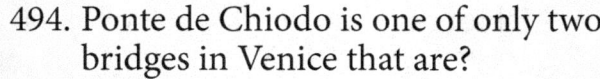

496. Isola Della Certosa is a Venetian Island that is often overlooked. What sets it apart?

a. Serenity in the form of nature
b. Water sports
c. It offers a break from the crowds
d. All the above

497. Which of the following is true of San Francesco Della Vigna?

a. It's a monastery
b. Silence is enforced
c. It has detailed frescos
d. All of the above

498. Why was Basilica d'Oro the original name of St. Mark's Basilica?

a. It has over a thousand square meters of golden mosaic tiles.
b. It was the Basilica of the Doge.
c. It was a Basilica for the wealthy.
d. It was the church of the sea captains.

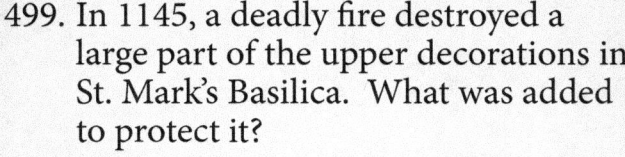

499. In 1145, a deadly fire destroyed a large part of the upper decorations in St. Mark's Basilica. What was added to protect it?
    a. Precious mosaic decorations
    b. Areas were covered in marble
    c. Old frescoes were covered over
    d. All the above

500. The clock tower in St. Mark's Piazza has something special that happens only twice a year? What is true of this special occasion?
    a. Three Magi emerge from the clock following Jesus the child.
    b. The first event is on January 6, Epiphany Day
    c. The second event is 40 days after Easter, the day Mary ascended in heaven
    d. All of the above

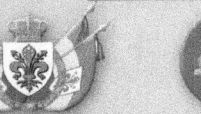

Answers - Venice Trivia

1. C	38. C	75. D	112. A	149. B	186. A	223. D
2. A	39. D	76. D	113. D	150. A	187. C	224. D
3. B	40. C	77. C	114. A	151. D	188. B	225. C
4. B	41. C	78. A	115. D	152. B	189. D	226. D
5. D	42. D	79. D	116. A	153. D	190. D	227. C
6. D	43. C	80. B	117. D	154. D	191. B	228. C
7. B	44. B	81. D	118. B	155. B	192. A	229. D
8. A	45. D	82. D	119. C	156. A	193. D	230. B
9. B	46. C	83. B	120. A	157. D	194. C	231. C
10. A	47. A	84. C	121. A	158. A	195. D	232. D
11. C	48. B	85. D	122. A	159. B	196. D	233. D
12. B	49. D	86. B	123. D	160. C	197. D	234. C
13. C	50. D	87. A	124. B	161. A	198. D	235. B
14. B	51. B	88. C	125. A	162. C	199. B	236. D
15. C	52. C	89. C	126. D	163. B	200. A	237. D
16. B	53. B	90. A	127. D	164. B	201. C	238. D
17. A	54. B	91. C	128. A	165. B	202. C	239. A
18. C	55. B	92. A	129. B	166. B	203. B	240. B
19. B	56. C	93. D	130. D	167. C	204. C	241. A
20. D	57. B	94. C	131. C	168. A	205. A	242. D
21. D	58. D	95. A	132. A	169. A	206. A	243. D
22. B	59. C	96. D	133. D	170. B	207. B	244. C
23. D	60. B	97. A	134. A	171. C	208. C	245. C
24. B	61. D	98. B	135. A	172. C	209. D	246. D
25. A	62. D	99. D	136. C	173. B	210. B	247. B
26. C	63. A	100. A	137. C	174. B	211. C	248. A
27. B	64. C	101. A	138. D	175. C	212. C	249. B
28. C	65. D	102. C	139. D	176. D	213. D	250. A
29. D	66. B	103. D	140. C	177. C	214. B	251. C
30. A	67. C	104. B	141. D	178. A	215. D	252. C
31. D	68. B	105. C	142. A	179. D	216. D	253. A
32. C	69. A	106. C	143. A	180. D	217. C	254. A
33. C	70. A	107. A	144. B	181. B	218. A	255. C
34. C	71. C	108. C	145. C	182. D	219. D	256. B
35. B	72. D	109. A	146. A	183. C	220. D	257. C
36. D	73. A	110. D	147. A	184. A	221. B	258. B
37. B	74. C	111. B	148. C	185. C	222. D	259. B

Answers - Venice Trivia

260. A	297. D	334. D	371. C	408. B	445. D	482. D
261. C	298. B	335. A	372. A	409. C	446. D	483. C
262. D	299. A	336. C	373. C	410. B	447. C	484. D
263. B	300. C	337. A	374. C	411. C	448. C	485. D
264. A	301. B	338. D	375. A	412. B	449. D	486. B
265. B	302. A	339. C	376. D	413. C	450. D	487. C
266. C	303. B	340. B	377. A	414. D	451. C	488. D
267. B	304. B	341. D	378. B	415. D	452. B	489. B
268. D	305. C	342. A	379. C	416. C	453. C	490. D
269. B	306. B	343. C	380. A	417. D	454. D	491. D
270. A	307. C	344. D	381. C	418. A	455. D	492. D
271. C	308. B	345. B	382. A	419. B	456. D	493. A
272. B	309. C	346. B	383. D	420. A	457. C	494. B
273. D	310. C	347. C	384. B	421. D	458. B	495. D
274. A	311. D	348. A	385. A	422. C	459. C	496. D
275. A	312. B	349. C	386. C	423. C	460. B	497. D
276. B	313. C	350. A	387. C	424. C	461. D	498. A
277. A	314. A	351. B	388. C	425. D	462. D	499. D
278. A	315. C	352. B	389. A	426. D	463. B	500. D
279. C	316. B	353. B	390. D	427. D	464. C	
280. A	317. D	354. D	391. B	428. D	465. A	
281. C	318. B	355. B	392. D	429. C	466. B	
282. B	319. D	356. C	393. A	430. D	467. C	
283. A	320. A	357. D	394. C	431. C	468. D	
284. C	321. D	358. D	395. C	432. D	469. B	
285. A	322. B	359. A	396. D	433. D	470. C	
286. D	323. C	360. C	397. B	434. D	471. D	
287. B	324. B	361. D	398. D	435. C	472. C	
288. C	325. D	362. B	399. D	436. D	473. D	
289. A	326. C	363. D	400. D	437. B	474. C	
290. C	327. A	364. C	401. B	438. A	475. C	
291. A	328. B	365. D	402. C	439. C	476. B	
292. C	329. C	366. B	403. A	440. D	477. D	
293. C	330. C	367. D	404. D	441. D	478. A	
294. D	331. C	368. C	405. C	442. A	479. D	
295. B	332. B	369. B	406. B	443. D	480. D	
296. A	333. B	370. A	407. D	444. D	481. C	

Worksheet

1.__☐	38.__☐	75.__☐	112.__☐	149.__☐	186.__☐	223.__☐
2.__☐	39.__☐	76.__☐	113.__☐	150.__☐	187.__☐	224.__☐
3.__☐	40.__☐	77.__☐	114.__☐	151.__☐	188.__☐	225.__☐
4.__☐	41.__☐	78.__☐	115.__☐	152.__☐	189.__☐	226.__☐
5.__☐	42.__☐	79.__☐	116.__☐	153.__☐	190.__☐	227.__☐
6.__☐	43.__☐	80.__☐	117.__☐	154.__☐	191.__☐	228.__☐
7.__☐	44.__☐	81.__☐	118.__☐	155.__☐	192.__☐	229.__☐
8.__☐	45.__☐	82.__☐	119.__☐	156.__☐	193.__☐	230.__☐
9.__☐	46.__☐	83.__☐	120.__☐	157.__☐	194.__☐	231.__☐
10.__☐	47.__☐	84.__☐	121.__☐	158.__☐	195.__☐	232.__☐
11.__☐	48.__☐	85.__☐	122.__☐	159.__☐	196.__☐	233.__☐
12.__☐	49.__☐	86.__☐	123.__☐	160.__☐	197.__☐	234.__☐
13.__☐	50.__☐	87.__☐	124.__☐	161.__☐	198.__☐	235.__☐
14.__☐	51.__☐	88.__☐	125.__☐	162.__☐	199.__☐	236.__☐
15.__☐	52.__☐	89.__☐	126.__☐	163.__☐	200.__☐	237.__☐
16.__☐	53.__☐	90.__☐	127.__☐	164.__☐	201.__☐	238.__☐
17.__☐	54.__☐	91.__☐	128.__☐	165.__☐	202.__☐	239.__☐
18.__☐	55.__☐	92.__☐	129.__☐	166.__☐	203.__☐	240.__☐
19.__☐	56.__☐	93.__☐	130.__☐	167.__☐	204.__☐	241.__☐
20.__☐	57.__☐	94.__☐	131.__☐	168.__☐	205.__☐	242.__☐
21.__☐	58.__☐	95.__☐	132.__☐	169.__☐	206.__☐	243.__☐
22.__☐	59.__☐	96.__☐	133.__☐	170.__☐	207.__☐	244.__☐
23.__☐	60.__☐	97.__☐	134.__☐	171.__☐	208.__☐	245.__☐
24.__☐	61.__☐	98.__☐	135.__☐	172.__☐	209.__☐	246.__☐
25.__☐	62.__☐	99.__☐	136.__☐	173.__☐	210.__☐	247.__☐
26.__☐	63.__☐	100.__☐	137.__☐	174.__☐	211.__☐	248.__☐
27.__☐	64.__☐	101.__☐	138.__☐	175.__☐	212.__☐	249.__☐
28.__☐	65.__☐	102.__☐	139.__☐	176.__☐	213.__☐	250.__☐
29.__☐	66.__☐	103.__☐	140.__☐	177.__☐	214.__☐	251.__☐
30.__☐	67.__☐	104.__☐	141.__☐	178.__☐	215.__☐	252.__☐
31.__☐	68.__☐	105.__☐	142.__☐	179.__☐	216.__☐	253.__☐
32.__☐	69.__☐	106.__☐	143.__☐	180.__☐	217.__☐	254.__☐
33.__☐	70.__☐	107.__☐	144.__☐	181.__☐	218.__☐	255.__☐
34.__☐	71.__☐	108.__☐	145.__☐	182.__☐	219.__☐	256.__☐
35.__☐	72.__☐	109.__☐	146.__☐	183.__☐	220.__☐	257.__☐
36.__☐	73.__☐	110.__☐	147.__☐	184.__☐	221.__☐	258.__☐
37.__☐	74.__☐	111.__☐	148.__☐	185.__☐	222.__☐	259.__☐

You can copy both sides of this worksheet and use it to record your answers. Then check off the correct answers by folding alongside the column and holding next to the Answer Sheet.

Worksheet

260.__☐	297.__☐	334.__☐	371.__☐	408.__☐	445.__☐	482.__☐
261.__☐	298.__☐	335.__☐	372.__☐	409.__☐	446.__☐	483.__☐
262.__☐	299.__☐	336.__☐	373.__☐	410.__☐	447.__☐	484.__☐
263.__☐	300.__☐	337.__☐	374.__☐	411.__☐	448.__☐	485.__☐
264.__☐	301.__☐	338.__☐	375.__☐	412.__☐	449.__☐	486.__☐
265.__☐	302.__☐	339.__☐	376.__☐	413.__☐	450.__☐	487.__☐
266.__☐	303.__☐	340.__☐	377.__☐	414.__☐	451.__☐	488.__☐
267.__☐	304.__☐	341.__☐	378.__☐	415.__☐	452.__☐	489.__☐
268.__☐	305.__☐	342.__☐	379.__☐	416.__☐	453.__☐	490.__☐
269.__☐	306.__☐	343.__☐	380.__☐	417.__☐	454.__☐	491.__☐
270.__☐	307.__☐	344.__☐	381.__☐	418.__☐	455.__☐	492.__☐
271.__☐	308.__☐	345.__☐	382.__☐	419.__☐	456.__☐	493.__☐
272.__☐	309.__☐	346.__☐	383.__☐	420.__☐	457.__☐	494.__☐
273.__☐	310.__☐	347.__☐	384.__☐	421.__☐	458.__☐	495.__☐
274.__☐	311.__☐	348.__☐	385.__☐	422.__☐	459.__☐	496.__☐
275.__☐	312.__☐	349.__☐	386.__☐	423.__☐	460.__☐	497.__☐
276.__☐	313.__☐	350.__☐	387.__☐	424.__☐	461.__☐	498.__☐
277.__☐	314.__☐	351.__☐	388.__☐	425.__☐	462.__☐	499.__☐
278.__☐	315.__☐	352.__☐	389.__☐	426.__☐	463.__☐	500.__☐
279.__☐	316.__☐	353.__☐	390.__☐	427.__☐	464.__☐	
280.__☐	317.__☐	354.__☐	391.__☐	428.__☐	465.__☐	
281.__☐	318.__☐	355.__☐	392.__☐	429.__☐	466.__☐	
282.__☐	319.__☐	356.__☐	393.__☐	430.__☐	467.__☐	
283.__☐	320.__☐	357.__☐	394.__☐	431.__☐	468.__☐	
284.__☐	321.__☐	358.__☐	395.__☐	432.__☐	469.__☐	
285.__☐	322.__☐	359.__☐	396.__☐	433.__☐	470.__☐	
286.__☐	323.__☐	360.__☐	397.__☐	434.__☐	471.__☐	
287.__☐	324.__☐	361.__☐	398.__☐	435.__☐	472.__☐	
288.__☐	325.__☐	362.__☐	399.__☐	436.__☐	473.__☐	
289.__☐	326.__☐	363.__☐	400.__☐	437.__☐	474.__☐	
290.__☐	327.__☐	364.__☐	401.__☐	438.__☐	475.__☐	
291.__☐	328.__☐	365.__☐	402.__☐	439.__☐	476.__☐	
292.__☐	329.__☐	366.__☐	403.__☐	440.__☐	477.__☐	
293.__☐	330.__☐	367.__☐	404.__☐	441.__☐	478.__☐	
294.__☐	331.__☐	368.__☐	405.__☐	442.__☐	479.__☐	
295.__☐	332.__☐	369.__☐	406.__☐	443.__☐	480.__☐	
296.__☐	333.__☐	370.__☐	407.__☐	444.__☐	481.__☐